Listen to My Case!

Listen to My Case!

When Women Approach the Courts of Tamil Nadu

Justice K. Chandru
Former Judge, Madras High Court

LeftWord

First published in February 2021.
Reprinted August 2021, November 2021.

LeftWord Books
2254/2A Shadi Khampur
New Ranjit Nagar
New Delhi 110008
INDIA

LeftWord Books and Vaam Prakashan are the publishing divisions of Naya Rasta Publishers Pvt. Ltd.

leftword.com

ISBN 978-81-944759-3-4 (paperback)
978-81-947287-7-1 (e-book)

Printed and bound by Chaman Enterprises, Delhi

Contents

Right to life, choice and dignity: Mapping personal journeys

Introduction

I began reading this book—about people who seek justice in courts—with high expectations. K. Chandru has spent a lifetime helping people who somehow find their way to the courts. As a judge in the Madras High Court, K. Chandru showed us what it is to be a judge of integrity;* what it is to practise judicial accountability; and what it is to be hard-working, passing orders on a record number of cases. Most of all, he is a person who has lived his commitment to justice for everyone. His landmark judgments have made a difference in many ways: among these are rulings on common burial grounds irrespective of caste; community-based reservation in noon meal centres; women becoming priests in temples; and doing away with police permission to stage plays.†

* Getting rid of some of the paraphernalia of the court system, one of the first things he did after becoming a judge was to dispense with the red-capped mace-bearer, who could be seen on the portals accompanying judges to their courts and chambers. He also found a sub-inspector-ranked personal security officer assigned to him redundant, and promptly discontinued the practice. Here was a judge who did not want his arrival announced by the silver-mace bearing 'Dawali'—a symbol of Power and Authority. He did not want a red beacon on his car; he did not want to be addressed as 'My Lord' in court; he did not accept any post-retirement jobs such as membership of tribunals and commissions, etc. He was the first judge to declare his assets to the Chief Justice at the time of appointment and again on the day of his retirement. A notice at the entrance of his official chamber read: 'No deities—No flowers, No one is hungry—No fruits, No one is shivering—No shawls'. (http://www.milligazette.com/news/6957-justice-chandru-may-your-tribe-increase)

† In *N.V. Sankaran Alias Gnani vs. The State Of Tamil Nadu* on 23 January

I was right to have expectations, because they were fully met. So vivid are the women in the book as they resist inequality through the court, that I found myself re-living my own legal encounter in the nineties. I recalled the moment when I made a shocking discovery—that in the eyes of the law, I was not the natural guardian of my minor son. With the help of Indira Jaising and the Women's Rights Initiative programme of the Lawyers Collective, my child's father and I filed a writ petition in the Supreme Court challenging the constitutional validity of the Hindu Minority and Guardianship Act (1956). Section 6 of this Act states that the mother is the natural guardian of her legitimate minor child 'after' the father; Section 19 of the Guardians and Wards Act (1890) debars the court from appointing the guardian of a minor whose father is living, and is not, in the court's opinion, unfit to be a guardian. Together, these sections were usually interpreted by the courts to mean that the child's welfare 'rests' with the father. The result: the mother is stripped of her right to be an equal partner in parenthood. The crux of our writ petition was the question, what disqualifies a mother from making decisions about her child's welfare? There is no social, economic, scientific or biological basis to the assumption that a woman is not capable of guardianship. And if there is no rational basis to this law, what is the sole criterion at work? The mother's gender. Did this not violate the equality promised by Articles 14 and 15 of the Constitution?

On 17 February 1999 a Supreme Court bench including

2013, Justice Chandru held that the provision to seek police permissions to stage plays was to be revoked, declaring certain provisions of Tamil Nadu Performance Act, 1954 as unconstitutional. As the petitioner had argued, '1954 Act was a relic of colonial rule in the country during which the Dramatic Performance Act, 1876, was enacted to regulate theatre. Though the law purported to grant an opportunity of hearing before an order of prohibition could be passed, such a procedure was an empty formality.' (https://indiankanoon.org/doc/182663805/)

the Chief Justice of India, wrote a judgment about mothers and children. The apex court ruled[‡] that 'it is an axiomatic truth that both the mother and father of a minor child are duty-bound to take due care of the person and the property of their child'. In a concurrent judgment, one of the members of the same bench noted that 'the father by reason of a dominant personality cannot be ascribed to have a preferential right over the mother in the matter of guardianship since both fall within the same category'.[§]

This was supposed to be a landmark judgment; a milestone in the struggle for women's rights. I should have felt some sense of triumph. But the truth that I could not overlook was a simple question: Are we so blind that we need the law to tell us a mother has the right to be her child's acknowledged guardian? But I realized, later, that re-reading the law, even in modest ways, means that a door is unlocked for other women to open wide.

In the India we want to re-make, in the world we aspire to, access to justice through the courts is for everyone. This is what we are working towards: a country where laws are made, read and applied so that justice is like air and water, essential nourishment for the community, and even that diverse thing, the nation. Once we have agreed on this, it may seem facetious to ask who should benefit from the law as practised by the courts. Sadly, the question needs to be asked again and again. The obvious answer is, of course, everyone in the country; but this answer is, too often, not part of lived experience. In this book, K. Chandru begins each of his stories—of actual cases—with reality that falls short of the justice promised to all citizens of India. Much of *Listen to My Case!*

‡ Paragraph 18 in *Ms. Githa Hariharan & Anr. vs. Reserve Bank Of India & Anr.* on 17 February 1999, https://indiankanoon.org/doc/1241462/

§ Paragraph 24 in *Ms. Githa Hariharan & Anr. vs. Reserve Bank Of India & Anr.* on 17 February 1999.

focuses on individual women who go to the courts, often against great odds.

From the mid-seventies, K. Chandru tells us, women began, slowly, and with difficulty, to approach the courts for remedy in a wide range of matters, from family property disputes to discrimination and harassment, to marital discord and violence. The stories Chandru recounts in this book—most of them set in Tamil Nadu—cover all aspects of lived experience. And they include the swathe of class, caste and community that make up Indian women. What brings this heterogeneous group together is their bravery in going to court, and their belief that the court—and society—owe them justice.

Consider: Amutha, whose husband had initiated a divorce, raised the question of whether her ten-year-old son could be examined in court to give evidence in favour of one parent. Muhabath Beevi, who was arrested during her Iddath period at 4.30 AM in the morning, went to court and won a public apology from an errant police officer. Kalithai, a coolie, lost her husband when he was taken to the police station—the police claimed his death was suicide. But though it took many years, the court finally ruled that it was a custodial death and that the state government should pay her compensation. Pothumallee saw how Dalit women were discriminated against when filling posts in noon meal centres and Anganwadi centres. She filed a writ petition to insist that reservation be applied while making these appointments.

These are just a few of the individuals we meet in the book, brave women all. Brave—because the process of going to court is hard; even harder when the woman is without financial or emotional support from family, custom, or the present reading of the law. Indeed, one of the women, Asan Banu, was also charged with going to court 'without permission'. Yet, in all the cases, the women display great personal courage; equally admirable and moving is the insistence on their right to legal justice. What also sets this collection of real women's stories apart is that in almost all the cases, there is victory as well, even if it is, on occasion, a pyrrhic victory.

This is a book that will speak powerfully to every woman, and everyone who abhors gender-based discrimination. But the book does more. Individual struggles shine like lone brave stars; but they are not really alone. Not far from them, there are several collective fights for justice. Whether it is a group, an entire village, a caste, a community, or a movement, these collective efforts shine like constellations. Their bold patterns bring people together, even those people who are supposedly powerless. Together they signal clearly: We will fight for our rights.

The book recalls a few well-known instances when the collective fight led to movements and, subsequently, to changes in the law. In 1972, Mathura, a young Adivasi, was called—illegally—to the police station after dark, and she was raped in custody. The courts did not exactly cover themselves in glory in this case: in 1979, the Supreme Court overturned the Bombay High Court judgment on the rapists' guilt, and said there were no marks of struggle on Mathura, and that she was 'habituated' to sex. The case caused outrage among many citizens, and various women's organizations were formed as a result of people rallying around Mathura. In addition to increasing awareness on women's legal rights and the ways in which patriarchy operates, mobilizing people also paved the way for a legal milestone on custodial rape.

The other milestone for women and the law was the Vishaka judgment in 1997. Vishaka, a women's rights group, along with some activists, filed a Public Interest Litigation (PIL) subsequent to the gang rape of a social service worker in Rajasthan. The PIL underlined the need for legal provisions that would address sexual harassment of women at the workplace. In this case, the court's judgment was a significant step ahead for gender equality, though it took till 2013 for Parliament to enact the law.

But this book, quite rightly, concerns itself with the lesser-known cases—what may seem 'small' or 'local' collective efforts. In reality, these are as important as the 'national'-level cases. And several of them illustrate that the fight for gender equality is a natural ally with the fight against caste, class and communal divisions.

The struggle against caste has to be on many levels, but it is important for the courts to adapt the use of laws to the ways in which discrimination and brutality occur every day in different settings. In one case, the people of Pothumbu village came together to protest the sexual harassment of schoolgirls by the headmaster of the government high school. With the support of a women's organization, their case resulted in a thorough inquiry, as well as a High Court judgment that addressed caste, and also the treatment of survivors. There are other cases K. Chandru has written of elsewhere, cases that affect women, but also the larger community. In a village called Sivanthipatti, Dalit agricultural labourers gained a victory in their daily struggle against caste discrimination. Many of them took the bus to Thirunelveli so they could sell their produce there. The bus service to their area was stopped; the High Court was shocked by the reason given by the police commissioner: If the bus stopped at the Dalit colony, all seats would be taken, and the townspeople—or caste Hindus—would have to stand. The court issued directions to resume the service to the Dalit colony bus stop. Another case challenged the caste-based segregation of people even after death. Despite the High Court's ruling that caste-wise allotment in the burial ground would be contrary to the right to equality and the abolition of untouchability, the practice continues. Beyond these small and big victories, there is so much still to be done.

But the fight is on, even if it means facing one obstacle after another; even if takes many long years. That's the news we get from this book, news from real people, whether it is women, or Dalits, or 'denotified tribes', or the mothers of activists who have been killed in police custody.

The book offers more: it reminds us that law is not static. The law comes alive every time it is re-read, re-interpreted to include the rights of more people in more situations; and when it responds to the questions and issues people raise—through resistance to inequality in specific situations. It's not just the people who benefit then. Public awareness, and informed public opinion enrich the reading of the law, and institutions such as courts, which are there to create and deliver justice to all citizens. Yes, this book presents numerous instances of inequality out of which many vicious situations arise. But really, this is a book which offers hope. When the law becomes rigid, and disconnected from real people; when justice is not within reach of every citizen because the authorities who should deliver it fail; the only place to find meaning in law, court and justice is in the determination of people to make laws inclusive, sensitive, progressive. This is what this book shows us so well. Hope lies in each of the brave people we meet in their moment of great adversity, and in their moment of struggle in the court. Hope lies in the fact that sometimes, even many times, their voices are heard. It is they who change their lives and ours for the better. The law, the court, are only the means.

Githa Hariharan

New Delhi
January 2020

Prologue

C.B. Muthamma, a senior Indian Foreign Service officer was not promoted to 'grade I' of the Service, while officers junior to her were promoted over her head. She waited for long, and in the end—that is, in the late-1970s—she knocked on the doors of the Supreme Court.

It was her good fortune that her case came before a bench that included the legendary Justice V.R. Krishna Iyer. The Court asked the Central Government why she was not given her due.

Try guessing the government's reply.

'Muthamma is single. If she was appointed as an ambassador, being a single woman she cannot entertain guests of State. So the Government does not appoint unmarried women IFS officers to independent posts.' It was strange that the rule did not apply to unmarried male officers.

Muthamma was the first woman to join the Indian Civil Service through the UPSC exam, which she cleared in 1948. It follows that she was the first woman to join the IFS. At the time of joining she was made to submit a written undertaking that she would resign in the event of her marriage. Perversely, her compliance with this rule had been held against her.

The judges were shocked by the government's reply. They warned that if Muthamma was not appointed ambassador forthwith, they would be compelled to declare the government's rules as unconstitutional.

By the next hearing, Muthamma was posted as ambassador to the Hague.

While closing the petition, Justice Krishna Iyer wrote in his judgment, 'We dismiss the petition, not the problem.'

Once described as a Young Turk, Nandini Satpathy was a senior Congress leader and former chief minister of Odisha. She resigned office in 1976, during the Emergency. While she was on the Opposition benches, a police officer once summoned her in the evening for questioning. She approached the Supreme Court, pleading that it was wrong to summon a woman to the police station after dark.

Section 160 of the Criminal Procedure Code provides that no woman shall be summoned to the police station; in particular she cannot be questioned at any place other than where she resides. The Supreme Court held that on no account could a woman be called to the police station after dark. It took this judgment to remind the police that such a provision existed in the books.

Around the same time, in September 1979, the Supreme Court acquitted an accused who had been convicted by the Sessions Court, in a case where a woman called Mathura had been gang raped. The reason for its decision was bewildering. The Court reasoned that there were no injury marks on Mathura's body. 'If she had fought against the rape, there would have been some injuries; because there are no injuries, it is concluded that she consented to the intercourse.'

Women's organizations all over the country rose in indignation. One heard cries of 'The court which granted justice to Muthamma and Nandini Satpathy, where are you?' Beginning December 1983, Parliament enacted many amendments in the provisions relating to rape.

It is now a hundred and fifty years since High Courts were

established in India. Yet, it was only after the United Nations's declaration of the International Year of Women in 1975 that women began to approach the courts for remedies to their problems. Societal evils relating to women began to be exposed as women increasingly began to invoke the law to protect themselves.

Family property disputes, marital discord, problems at work, harassment, and gender discrimination were among the many reasons women went to court.

Violence against women continues. Why don't all women rise against it and fight their battles in court? The majority of women submit to injustice because they are faced with the question: 'When we are afraid of confronting our husband and family in private, how can we think of approaching the courts?'

In the face of extreme cruelty, there are some women who bravely seek legal recourse. Such women as Pinnaiyakkal, Tamilarasi and Asan Banu, who have fought injustice and triumphed in court, stand as examples of courage before us.

The stories of a few such dauntless women are narrated here. Many sagas of fearlessness have faded without being recorded. Some day, they will have to be recovered. For readers who want to see the text of an order passed by me, the relevant references to the cases/reported references in the law journals are provided at the end of each story.

My sincere thanks and gratitude must go to Githa Hariharan, my longtime friend. She was kind enough to give her foreword, with liberal usage of phrases to commend my work and service. Not stopping with that, she also gave useful suggestions for shaping the book. She also helped in getting the valuable services of Salim Yusufji and Abhilasha Chattopadhyay of the Indian Writers Forum who did an excellent job in editing my book and bringing it to the present shape. I will be failing in my duty if I do not acknowledge my friend and colleague in the Bench, Justice Prabha Sridevan who suggested the English version of this book and also made the first draft of the manuscript.

Justice K. Chandru — Chennai

January 2020

Life after loss

Kalithai

The police force is a fence formed to protect public rights. But if the fence becomes an enabler of violation, what is to be done? This is the story of Kalithai who fought a legal battle against such violation.

Kalithai and her husband Marisamy worked as coolies. They lived in the village of Nelkattumseval in Thirunelveli district, Tamil Nadu. The inspector of police at the Vasudevanallur station arrested three men—Marisamy, Ramar and Murugaiah—on 16 September 1998, and brought them to the Sankarankoil Police Station at 9.30 AM. They waited in the writer's room for their interrogation. The police did not note their arrest in the station register. Then, Marisamy went to the toilet and did not return.

The inspector had left the police station but when he returned at 12 noon he was informed that Marisamy was lying dead in the toilet. The constables said he had tied his lungi into a knot and hung himself in the toilet. Because the death had occurred in the police station, as per Police Standing Order No. 145 the Thirunelveli revenue divisional officer was informed of the matter. After conducting an inquiry, the RDO sent a report on 12 March 1999 stating that because the police officers had reprimanded him, Marisamy killed himself out of a sense of humiliation. The district collector duly forwarded the report to the government.

Kalithai sent a letter to the Chief Justice of the Madras High Court seeking justice for the death of her husband. The Chief

Justice ordered that the letter be treated as a writ petition. A notice was issued to the government. Kalithai, who was unaware of all this, also sent a complaint to the National Human Rights Commission (NHRC). Apart from this, she filed a case in 1999 seeking compensation for Marisamy's death.

In the meantime the Tamil Nadu government, which examined the report of the RDO, issued a government order (GO) on 4 February 2000. It said that while Marisamy had committed suicide, his arrest was not recorded in the station register by the police, who, after taking him into custody, also allowed him to remain in a lungi; in effect, they had facilitated the suicide. It held them responsible for the two lapses. Further, the GO ordered a departmental inquiry to be initiated against Vijaya Raghavan (inspector, Vasudevanallur), Kottaisamy (sub-inspector), Samuthiravel (head constable), Venkatachalam and Kasipandian (grade I police constables) and Solaisamy (assistant station writer). Thereafter, the district police superintendent of Thirunelveli conducted disciplinary proceedings against the accused policemen, and after imposing the minor punishment of a reduction in pay, closed the file.

To the NHRC, the Tamil Nadu government replied that action had been taken against the errant policemen. The government thereby stalled further proceedings in the NHRC. Kalithai was to receive a further shock. The High Court, which had treated her letter as a writ petition, had appointed a legal aid counsel for her. When her case finally came up for hearing—on 13 June 2006, seven years after it was filed—the Division Bench dismissed the case for default because of the counsel's non-appearance at the proceedings. The court noted:

After treating it as a writ petition, no notice was sent to the

> petitioner. However, an Advocate of this Court was appointed as an amicus curiae to assist the Court. Unfortunately, when the matter came up before the Division Bench on 13.6.2005, the said amicus curiae had not appeared. No further intimation was ... sent to the petitioner. Further, the Division bench was also not informed about the pendency of the writ petition having been filed by the petitioner herself in ... 1999 and prosecuted by an Advocate. In the absence of such information, the Division bench dismissed the writ petition for default vide its order dated 13.6.2005.

Kalithai, who did not know any of this, waited ten years, hoping for justice. The other petition Kalithai had filed in 1999, for compensation, came before a single judge in 2009. The government counsel informed the court that since a Division Bench had already dismissed the case filed in her name, no relief could be granted in this proceeding. The single judge who looked at the records saw that an injustice had been done to Kalithai and requested the Chief Justice to place the matter before a new Division Bench. Accordingly, the case was listed before another Division Bench. The government filed a counter affidavit that since Marisamy had committed suicide, there was no provision in the law to give Kalithai compensation as per the GO of the year 1998 which ensures a financial relief of one lakh rupees, sanctioned by the government in cases of death in caste/communal clashes, death due to police torture, death due to police firing, rape committed by police.

The Division Bench was headed by Justice P.K. Misra. Not only did the Division Bench severely reprimand the government counsel, it also held that the police department had erred in not recording the arrest of Marisamy in the station register, and the entire responsibility for his death fell on the police since he had died in custody. Moreover, since the Tamil Nadu Government itself had conducted a departmental inquiry which held the policemen responsible for Marisamy's death, the Bench decided that the government should bear responsibility for the custodial death and pay a sum of Rs. 2 lakhs as compensation within two months. The Court severely reprimanded the conduct of the policemen.

Reference:

M. Kalithai vs. State of Tamil Nadu, 2009 (3) MLJ 702 (DB)

A mother's oath

A theatre group called Marappachi, led by A. Mangai, staged two plays in April 2013, *Vakkumoolam* (Confessions) and *Sudalaiammal*, both scripted by V. Geetha. The two plays had as their theme the excesses committed in Tamil Nadu during the Emergency, between 1975 and 1977. A guard at the burial ground in a village in North Arcot (present-day Thiruvannamalai and Vellore districts), Sudalaiammal performs the last rituals for corpses, according dignity to the dead. One day a young man's body is brought there by some policemen, the body covered in injuries. The policemen want to have it burned at once. But the mother's heart recognizes the dead youth. Not heeding their warnings that she should not tell anyone about this incident, Sudalaiammal performs the last rites, then narrates the whole truth about the young man to reporters before going to sleep. With that the play ends. Revathi's acting brought Sudalaiammal to life before the audience.

Sudalaiammal is an imaginary character who narrates a true story, that of Seeralan, who lost his life to the police during the Emergency when such excesses had free rein. This character of Sudalaiammal was actually a combination of three real women. The first woman is Seeralan's mother Baggiam Duraiswamy. Baggiam is a homemaker and her husband, Duraiswamy, is an electricity board employee; for thirty years after the murder of their son Seeralan, they fought for justice. Their legal battle started in 1976 and did not end till August 2006. The second woman is Jaya Velu who was an eyewitness to the torture inflicted on Seeralan. Fearing that they would tell the truth, the police department threatened poor Jaya and her husband, Velu. They inflicted untold torture on the couple and sent them to jail on a fabricated case. To date Jaya and Velu's whereabouts have not been discovered. The third woman is Mythily Sivaraman. She went to many villages and hamlets and collected information on the killing, staging fearless protests in her fight for justice. She also went up to the then Governor and made a representation that an inquiry should be conducted by a member of the revenue board. She may retain no memories of these incidents today because of age-related dementia, but in those days, in spite of the severe censorship that prevailed during the Emergency, she published a chilling article titled 'The Murder of Seeralan' in *Economic and Political Weekly* (24 September 1977) that was published from Bombay. Along with this article, many others that she had written in the 1970s have been published by LeftWord as a book titled *Haunted by Fire*. V. Geetha, who edited the book, spoke the day the play was staged and said it was Mythily Sivaraman's article that formed the crux of the play.

Let us turn to the legal battle fought by Seeralan's mother Baggiam Duraiswamy, for thirty years. Ponneri is a village in North Arcot. In 1976, farm workers there agitated for payment of the minimum wages announced for agricultural labourers by the Tamil Nadu government. It was Seeralan who gathered the agricultural labourers together and led the agitation. He was not even twenty years old. At the instigation of the landlords, the police arrested Seeralan and tortured him. They placed the yoke used for cattle on Seeralan's neck and see-sawed on it. No medical aid was given to him and on 11 January 1977 Seeralan died. The police fabricated a new story that Seeralan was a Naxalite who had attacked them when they went to arrest him and that they were compelled to kill him in self-defence. The Thirupathur Sub-Collector who conducted the autopsy condemned the police cruelty. He said that the three constables Kasinathan, Ramasamy and Sivalingam had tortured and killed Seeralan and attempted to conceal it, that action must be taken against them and also against the inspector and superintendent who had abetted the act. No action was taken on this report of 6 February 1977. Then, S.P. Srinivasan—an IAS officer and member of the revenue board—was asked to inquire into the matter. His inquiry report (May 1977) confirmed the Sub-Collector's report of February. Srinivasan recommended that criminal action should be taken against the policemen. The case was tried by the Vellore sessions judge, who accepted the case of the policemen and acquitted them, agreeing that they had acted in self-defence and Seeralan died as a consequence. Seeralan's mother, Baggiam, filed a revision petition against this, which was also dismissed.

Undeterred, Baggiam filed a second case in 1984, asking for compensation from the State for the custodial violence. This came up for hearing after another ten years, in 1994. Justice P.S. Mishra, who heard the case, held that though the criminal case was dismissed, its dismissal could not be the grounds for refusing to pay compensation. The court noted:

> The accused in criminal trial are acquitted not for the reason that the Court is not satisfied with the truth of the allegation, but because the prosecution has not been able to prove its case beyond a reasonable doubt. It is for this reason that the Court does not accept the decisions of the Criminal Courts as binding upon the Civil Courts.

Further, the judgment held:

The action for compensation has not arisen as a consequence of the conviction of the accused person. It has arisen on account of death, which, it is alleged, was caused by the police and if it is so, the State has a liability to compensate the petitioner.

Justice Mishra said that the violence inflicted on Seeralan was listed in the report filed by the IAS officer Srinivasan and his recommendations formed the basis of the criminal case. Legally and morally, the State was bound to pay compensation. He directed the payment of Rs. 1 lakh as compensation, adding that the sum be deposited in a bank and a monthly interest of not less than Rs. 1,000 be paid to Baggiam.[i] This was in 1994, when she was sixty. She filed an appeal stating that the compensation was too low. This came before a division bench headed by Chief Justice A.P. Shah. The Bench gave its judgment on 11 August 2006.[ii] Since Baggiam's petitions had asked for only Rs. 1 lakh the judges could not increase the compensation but since Justice Mishra's order of 1994 had not been implemented by the State, they said it was bound to pay the principal amount with interest for the delay of twelve years, an additional amount aggregating to Rs. 2.2 lakhs. The thirty-year battle against all trials and tribulations finally bore fruit and the mother triumphed.

References:

i) *Baggiam Doraiswamy vs. State of Tamil Nadu*, 1994 (2) LW (Crl.) 687

ii) *Baggiam Doraiswamy vs. State of Tamil Nadu*, W.A. No. 1929 of 2005, dt. 11.8.2006

Asan Banu

The king Ellalan, or 'Manuneethi Chozhan' as he is also called, ruled from Anuradhapura in present-day Sri Lanka, sometime during the third to second century BCE, and is the subject of much popular lore. These stories concern his fairness in settling disputes. He is believed to have once rendered justice to a cow that rang the Araichi Mani (a giant bell installed outside the king's courtroom) to complain that the king's son had driven his chariot over her calf. Our country has honoured this king by erecting his statue in the High Court campus, Chennai. Can we in the same country excuse an officer who persecuted a woman for going to court and seeking justice?

This is the story of Asan Banu.

Asan Banu's husband was a 'last grade servant' with the Madurai Corporation and lived with his family in a tenement belonging to the Corporation. On his sudden death, Asan Banu was employed on compassionate grounds as a 'park servant', but the Corporation asked Asan Banu to vacate the unit where she had continued to live after her husband's demise. Asan Banu approached the High Court at Chennai and obtained a stay against the eviction.

The administration was annoyed that she had had the temerity to move court against the Corporation. In retaliation, she was temporarily suspended from work and issued a show cause notice containing ten charges. One of the charges was peculiar: it accused her of going to court without obtaining permission. Another charge against her was of questioning the Commissioner's order.

This time Asan Banu did not have to travel to Chennai to challenge the order. On 24 July 2004, after twenty-five years of struggle, the Madurai bench had been inaugurated for the people of the southern districts of Tamil Nadu. The High Court issued a notice to the Commissioner, asking him to reply. The advocate who appeared for the Corporation could not justify its actions.

The High Court held that the disciplinary action taken against Asan Banu violated her fundamental rights under the Constitution; any local authority employee can approach the court to establish her right; no permission was required. The order reads:

> The petitioner had exercised her constitutional right of moving this court and getting her grievance redressed. The respondent cannot make that an excuse to frame a number of charges including the charge that she had moved the High Court, and browbeat her into meek submission. This Court takes a serious view of the conduct of the respondent in having framed the charges.

It further said that the Corporation's show cause notice to the worker was an obstruction of the legal process, and that the Court had the power to find the Commissioner in contempt and punish him. Though no individual action for contempt was initiated against the Commissioner, the Court imposed costs of Rs. 5,000 for threatening and intimidating a 'last grade worker' without justification, and for causing her a monetary loss by making her approach the Court a second time.

In general, when costs are imposed on superiors, they tend to be reluctant to pay up and may attempt to intimidate the complainant. To ascertain that the costs were paid in accordance with its final order, the Court listed the matter for three weeks later. The counsel for the Corporation now submitted that the Corporation had offered Asan Banu the money, but she had refused it. He produced a cheque drawn in favour of Asan Banu. The Court ordered her to appear before it. She came with her children, fear writ large on her face. She was apprehensive that there would be more problems if she took the money.

The Court explained to her that the money was the compensation paid to a successful party. Only if this was done would the authorities come to appreciate the fundamental rights of a citizen under the Constitution. The Court also told her that she could use the money to buy new clothes and sweets for her children in the coming Ramzan festival. At this she agreed to take it.

That day, the Indian flag on the High Court building seemed to flutter with a new pride.

The judgment held that the court was proud to ensure that the rights of a 'last grade female servant' of the Corporation were protected, adding that this case had justified the establishment of the Madurai bench.

Reference:

R. Asan Banu vs. Commissioner, Corporation of Madurai, 2007 (4) MLJ 1207

Malathi

Rice and vegetables I cooked and the smoke streamed out of the window,
But if I step out of my threshold, they call me a luckless widow.
To make my meal there is a stove, and the heat goes out of the window,
But where can I go out? They call me an ill-starred widow.

Thus goes a folk song which is the lament of a young widow.

The injustice inflicted on widows in our country is boundless. This is not a phenomenon which arose just a few centuries ago. Widows have been treated with cruelty right from the Sangam period (c. 3rd century BCE – 3rd century CE) which is praised as the golden age of the Tamils.

In an ancient Tamil text, *Purananuru*, the poet Aavoor Moolankizhar compares the loss of prosperity of the hero's house to the loss of beauty in a woman, who, on becoming a widow, appears without any ornaments and with a shaven head (verse 206). Again, in the *Purananuru*, the poet Thayankanniar describes the pitiful state of a newly-widowed woman who must shave her head and remove her bangles (verse 250).

The *Manushastra* lays downs the rules on what a widow can and cannot do.

> 5.157. At her pleasure let her emaciate her body by (living on) pure flowers, roots, and fruit; but she must never even mention the name of another man after her husband has died.
>
> 5.158. Until death let her be patient (of hardships), self-controlled, and chaste, and strive (to fulfil) that most excellent duty which (is prescribed) for wives who have one husband only.
>
> [...]
>
> 5.164. By violating her duty towards her husband, a wife is disgraced in this world, (after death) she enters the womb of a jackal, and is tormented by diseases (the punishment of) her sin.

In her book *Stri Purush Tulana*, the Marathi writer, Tarabai Shinde (1850–1910), listed the cruelties inflicted on women. She asked why the shastras and their rules burden women disproportionately with rules of conduct, and expressed anguish over the saying that not even a dog will touch the food eaten by a widow.

Many social reformers appeared in the nineteenth century, even before our freedom struggle. They raised the battle cry that Hindu society must remove the injustice done to widows. Pandit Ishwar Chandra Vidyasagar from Bengal, Veeresalingam Pantulu from South India, Justice Mahadev Govind Ranade from Maharashtra, Dayanand Saraswati from North India are some of the names of such reformers. They recommended the remarriage of widows.

The Constitution that was drafted after Independence declares in Article 39-A that the State is bound to protect the right to adequate livelihood of Indian citizens regardless of gender. After Indira Gandhi became prime minister, the Constitution was amended in 1976, introducing fundamental duties. In Article 51-

A(c), it is declared that all practices that are offensive to women's dignity must be abjured.

But the case filed by Assistant Inspector Malathi proves that even in the twenty-first century our attitude to widows has not changed. Malathi was appointed as first grade constable on 1 July 1977. She was promoted to head constable in 1986 and assistant inspector in 1994. In June 2005 she went on medical leave. Since the leave she applied for exceeded sixty days, she was sent to the medical board for inspection. After examining her, the board approved her leave till 22 December 2005. But she could not join work even after that. Since her husband had suffered a severe heart attack and was being treated at the Vellore Hospital, she applied for additional leave. But Malathi's husband died on 21 February 2006. As she was now a widow, her contact with the outside world was cut in accordance with religious customs. Although the police authorities knew of her husband's death, they declared her a deserter and removed her from service. She filed a review petition to the chief of the police department, stating that her husband had died of heart disease after prolonged treatment and as she belonged to the Brahmin community, her contact with the outside world had been severed in accordance with customs, and in these difficult circumstances she had not been able to resume duty. Without considering this explanation, the police department altered the punishment to one of compulsory retirement and closed the file.

Though she had lost her husband and her job, she courageously knocked on the doors of justice. The High Court took the case on file, summoned the relevant records and examined them. The High Court pointed out that not only had the department not considered the reasons given by her for not appearing on the dates fixed for the inquiry, but the department had also not considered her letter explaining her husband's health condition. The Court wondered how, even after offering their condolences to Malathi for her husband's death, the authorities could display such ignorance of the religious and traditional practices regarding widows and had declared her a deserter instead. The Court expressed its anguish that though the fundamental duties declared in our Constitution require us to give up customary practices against the dignity of women, the society has still not changed. The Court recorded the cruel social history regarding Hindu widows.

> The predicament of the petitioner will have to be seen in the above context of a long history of imposed isolation of the widow from society, and the customary duties to observe certain mandatory rituals. ... [T]he explanation offered by the petitioner cannot be brushed aside by the authorities. If the first respondent wanted to really show leniency, then he should have looked into the cause for her absence and cannot pass a mechanical order.

The judgment said that even if Malathi's failure to report to duty was a lapse, the department ought to have awarded a punishment proportionate to the lapse and not a disproportionately severe one. It severely condemned the police department for its action and ordered the immediate reinstatement of Malathi. The department implemented the order at once.

Malathi's courage in fighting her battle after losing her husband may well prove an inspiration to other women.

Reference:

R. Malathy vs. Director General of Police, Tamil Nadu, 2011 (5) CTC 829

Mother, mothering and motherhood

Amutha

Your children are not your children.
They are the sons and daughters of Life's longing for itself.
They come through you but not from you,
And though they are with you yet they belong not to you.

You may give them your love but not your thoughts,
For they have their own thoughts.
You may house their bodies but not their souls,
For their souls dwell in the house of tomorrow,
which you cannot visit, not even in your dreams.
You may strive to be like them, but seek not to make them
like you.
For life goes not backward nor tarries with yesterday.
You are the bows from which your children as living arrows
are sent forth.
Let your bending in the Archer's hand be for gladness . . .

In a case that came before the High Court, this poem by Khalil Gibran was quoted. It is a question that arises in many cases whether children can be examined as witnesses in a criminal case. The Supreme Court has held that it is permissible to record their evidence provided a conducive atmosphere is created for the minor to give it. Amutha raised this question in a matrimonial case, asking whether a child can be examined to give evidence in favour of one parent.

Seeking divorce, Amutha's husband had filed a case against her before the sub-court, Erode, in 2005. According to him, his wife had deserted him and he wanted his ten-year-old son Aravind to give evidence against the mother. The evidence of the child as Plaintiff's Witness 1 was filed in accordance with the Civil Procedure Code. (There is no provision in law for a minor—under eighteen—to swear to affidavits.) When her son stood in the witness box, Amutha refused to cross examine him and asked that his evidence not be taken on file. The learned sub-judge said that there is no legal bar against recording his evidence. The judge rejected her objections, stating that he was satisfied with the mental capability of the minor. Against this order of dismissal, Amutha filed a case before the High Court.

Though the law does not forbid child witnesses, it is a vexed question whether they should be examined as witnesses in matrimonial disputes, since the child is liable to lose either the father or the mother permanently. Therefore the High Court said that the child's evidence must not be taken on file.

> The competency of a person to sign an affirmative statement especially when the person is a child, . . . cannot be permitted since the child cannot be said to be a competent person to sign an affirmation. In fact, Section 3(3) of the General Clause Act defines an affidavit, which reads as follows: 'affidavit shall include affirmation and declaration in the case of persons by law allowed to affirm or declare instead of swearing'.

In this case, since Aravind resided with his father, the probability of his being influenced and tutored by the father could not be ruled out and in these circumstances he was not qualified to file an affidavit. The law says that an affidavit, which is a sworn statement, can be filed only by persons above eighteen years of age. The affidavit filed on Aravind's behalf stated facts that dated from before his birth. This confirmed the suspicion that he was under the control of his father. The court noted:

> [I]n fact, the affidavit itself clearly shows that he was aware of the fact that his father was filing a divorce application, and it uses language, mainly legal in nature, which is not expected of a child. The fact of ascertaining the mental capability of the child (11 years old) at the time of examination by the trial Judge, cannot take the case of the respondent any further.

The High Court therefore set aside the order of the sub-court and directed the court to proceed with the case while eschewing Aravind's evidence. It was only to stress the position that though children are born to parents, the parents do not have suzerainty over their children, that the poem by Khalil Gibran was quoted. Amutha lost the case. She was not permitted to see her child. Her only satisfaction was that, living in the same town, she was able to see her child grow up into an adult. This was her solace and also her heartache.

Reference:

S. Amutha vs. C. Manivanna Bhupathy, 2007 (1) MLJ 916 = 2007 (2) CTC 97

Kalaiselvi

Should one give birth to be a mother? It is not necessary. A person who adopts a child is equally a parent. This is what the Indian Adoption Act says. The Hindu religion also permits adoption, for continuation of the family and for succession to property. Before the 1956 Act came into force, when India was under British Rule, relief was given under the Guardians and Wards Act of 1890. On applying, widows were appointed as guardians of minors who were heirs to landed property. Though the Hindu religion permitted a childless widow to adopt, the colonial ruler played politics to deny the inheritance rights of Indians. The law allowed Hindus to adopt children with the consent of the biological parents, or orphaned children from their court-appointed guardian. In 2009, the Madras High Court ordered that Christian couples can also adopt. The Juvenile Justice Act, 2000, contains Section 41 that allows adoption without any discrimination of caste or creed. If one is unable to bear children and does not want to adopt children, one has the option of getting the help of a surrogate mother and to have children through surrogacy. The Surrogacy Regulation Bill, 2016, was passed on 19 December 2018 outlawing commercial surrogacy, limiting 'altruistic' surrogacy to family members, and setting a lifetime limit of one surrogate pregnancy per woman. The fertilized egg is implanted in the surrogate mother's womb and once the child is born, it belongs to the childless couple (homosexuals, live-in couples and single parents being excluded from the benefits of the Act). There are plenty of laws and decisions in western countries on the legal identity and status of the child but our Parliament has not come forward to enact a clear law regarding the rights of children born through surrogacy. There are many social complications because there is no legislative clarity regarding the inheritance rights of such a child and regarding the identity of the biological mother.

In 2009, a woman working in the Chennai Port Trust lost her only son, a twenty-year-old, in a road accident. Because she was biologically unable to bear children, she had a child through surrogacy on medical advice. She made a request to the management to nominate the child as her heir to receive the terminal benefits and a medical facilities card. The department said no, in view of the legal problems, and said that until the central government enacted a law no relief could be granted.

Moreover, the court referred to the averment made by the respondent:

> It is submitted that apart from legal, other issues such as moral, ethical, psychological and religious are involved in surrogacy procedure. Hence, in India a comprehensive legislation is very much the need of the hour to address the complex legal issues related to surrogacy.

Against this, the mother filed a case in the High Court. She contended that as the real mother of the child born through surrogacy she was entitled to all the rights and benefits that are given to adoptive parents. The Madras High Court granted her relief and ordered:

> The respondent Chennai Port Trust is directed to grant leave to the petitioner in terms of Rule 3-A recognising the child obtained through surrogate procedure. Further a direction is

> issued to the respondent to include the name of the child . . . as a member of the petitioner's family and also include her name in the FMI card forthwith.

A society which has accepted organ transplants should also come forward to accept children born through surrogacy.

Subsequently, in another case, the Bombay High Court also gave a similar judgment. The central government has also recognized its responsibility and come forward to give six months' pregnancy leave to government servants to bear children through surrogacy.

Reference:

K. Kalaiselvi vs. Chennai Port Trust, 2013 (2) CTC 400 = 2013 (3) MLJ 493

Karpagam/Sharmila

India is fast competing with China, though mostly in the growth of population. The old blessing that one must have many children is forgotten as we increasingly see government advertisements advising couples not to have more than one child.

During the Emergency (1975–77), on Sanjay Gandhi's instructions compulsory sterilization was performed on many persons in the North. Even unmarried young men could not escape the authorities who had steep vasectomy targets to meet. Totally rejecting the bid to control their bodies and fertility, the people of North India arose as one in rage and defeated Indira Congress by voting against her in the 1977 election. There can be no doubt that compulsory sterilization goes against human rights. In the field of reproductive choice the government's role has been despotic but inconsistent. In nineteenth-century England imprisonment was awarded to anybody who propagated birth control. In 1877, Annie Besant and Charles Bradlaugh were arrested for selling pamphlets promoting family planning. Immediately a criminal case was filed against her for spreading anti-God propaganda. Artificial birth control was considered as running contrary to the Christian faith. The traditional belief, supported by the authorities, was that childbirth was an act of God. In Ireland, the 2012 death of a woman of Indian origin, Savita Halappanavar, occurred because of a law based on religious belief which prevented her from receiving an abortion after an incomplete miscarriage. There was immense public anger after this incident, where a mother was allowed to die and all the focus was on saving the unborn child. Public opinion duly shifted and Ireland legalized abortion in December 2018.

The situation in our country is different. Alongside birth control propaganda we see the widespread practice of female foeticide. A large number of pregnancies are terminated after determining the sex of the unborn child. There is a proverb in Tamil that even a ruler will turn into a pauper if he has five daughters. Centres for sex determination have spread all over our country. Parliament has passed an Act forbidding sex determination tests. Yet, female foeticide and infanticide have increased. As a consequence the man-woman ratio, which could be 50:50, has now reduced in some regions to 800 women per 1,000 men. To prevent infanticide, the Tamil Nadu government started the Cradle Baby Scheme in 1992. At its start, many baby girls were anonymously left in the cradles. Numbers have fallen off lately. This does not mean that the practice of killing the girl child stopped. Even today sex determination clinics operate covertly. Ours must be the only country where attendants in government hospitals ask for a tip of Rs. 1,000 if a boy is born and Rs. 500 when it is a girl. To prevent female infanticide, the government of Tamil Nadu announced a girl-child protection scheme. As per this scheme, if a person agrees to be sterilized after the birth of two daughters, a bank deposit is created in each child's name and a sum of Rs. 15,000 put in each account. When the girl attains the age of eighteen years this deposit is given to her family, together with interest. If the couple undergoes procedures for birth control after just one daughter there is a bonus. The deposit in the name of the child goes up to Rs. 22,000. Under both these schemes, it is mandatory for the mother to undergo sterilization. This is because the government wanted to discourage the attempts of people to keep having babies till they get a boy.

In Thiruvidaimaruthur, one Karpagam gave birth to a daughter. She was called Bhuvaneswari. The second child was born in a private hospital. She was called Jayanthi. Karpagam immediately underwent sterilization. When she applied to join the girl-child protection scheme her application was rejected. They informed her that since her sterilization surgery was performed in a private hospital she was not entitled to join the scheme.

She filed a case before the High Court. Under the terms of the Tamil Nadu government scheme, there was nothing to indicate that going to a private hospital for delivery or birth control would result in disqualification. The High Court therefore ordered that Karpagam should get the benefit of the scheme.[i]

The court noted:

> In the rules referred to, there is no power vested with the third respondent the Commissioner, Panchayat Union to reject any application on his own. It is the District Social Welfare Officer who has to personally verify the details submitted by an applicant. ... The case pleaded by the petitioner comes within the scheme framed by the Government and the respondents cannot reject the same on a reason which is not found under the orders of the Government.

The state governments in India have adopted innovative methods to discourage large families. In 1993, the Haryana legislature made an amendment to the existing law, to the effect that a person who had more than two children could not stand for election to a local body. The case filed against this move was dismissed by the Supreme Court in 2003. It rejected the argument that a woman's pregnancy could be the result of sexual coercion; whereas the new law punished women and men alike. The Supreme Court asserted:

> In our view, disqualification on the right to contest an

election by having more than two living children does not contravene any fundamental right nor does it cross the limits of reasonability. Rather it is a disqualification conceptually devised in national interest.

In 1980 the Supreme Court had upheld a rule that air hostesses should not have children during the training period. In both judgments, the Supreme Court declared that these rules were introduced with women's health as the object.

It was on this basis that in 1997 the Tamil Nadu Government notified that leave with pay would not be granted for the birth of a third child. The Universal Declaration of Human Rights, adopted by the UN General Assembly in 1948, provides that it is a fundamental human right to receive care for motherhood. The International Labour Organization has also passed a resolution to protect childbearing women. The only country which has not given legal protection to women as per the above conventions is USA. Article 42 of our Constitution provides for maternity relief. In 1961, Parliament enacted the Maternity Benefit Act. Under the terms of this Act, a pregnant worker cannot be asked to work six weeks before delivery and six weeks after delivery, leave with pay should also be given for delivery, and a pregnant worker cannot be removed from work before delivery. Since women usually had children only after marriage, a multinational company, Pfizer, began terminating the employment of women as soon as they got married as per the contractual terms in the early '60s. This was because Pfizer thought that married women would take leave frequently to have children. The employees' challenge was negatived by the Industrial Tribunal, but later that Award was reversed by the Supreme Court. The Supreme Court criticized this practice and held that under the Maternity Benefit Act even if widows or unmarried girls have children, the benefits under the Act must be given to them. In 2008, a beedi company in Thirunelveli refused to give salary and leave to two women workers citing that the policy of the government was that no family should have more than two children. Bhadrakali and Santhammal[ii] approached the court and got relief by contending that the bar against having more than two children had not become law. The court highlighted the arguments of Mr. M. Muthupandian, learned counsel for the third respondent:

> MB [Maternity Benefit] Act does not provide any restriction on the benefit to be received by a woman worker if she delivers more than two times. The policy of the Government in having a two-child norm, cannot be read into the Act and whatever applies to a government servant need not be made applicable to the Beedi workers, who are governed by the provisions of MB Act. To show the difference between government servants and other workers, he also submitted that in respect of government servants, no Maternity Leave will be given if the marriage is preceded by delivery, whereas in the case of workers governed by the MB Act, even an unmarried female worker is entitled for the maternity benefit if she delivers a child.

The court further noted:

> There is no provision under the MB Act fixing any ceiling on the number of deliveries made by a female worker. So long as Article 42 of the Constitution read with the provisions of the MB Act is available, every female worker covered by the Act is entitled to claim maternity benefits without any ceiling on the number of deliveries made by them.

The following year, Sharmila,[iii] who worked as a trainee teacher in the Thoothukudi block development office had a different experience. The government refused to give her maternity benefit for the second delivery. She had had twins earlier. The government said that the second delivery was actually her third child and she was ineligible for leave with pay. She challenged the ruling before the High Court. The High Court referred to the history of laws relating to maternity benefits and the UN Convention regarding Maternity Protection and said that if the State intended to protect the second delivery, then the grounds that this was the third child were immaterial. The court noted:

> In the present case, it is sufficient to state that if the intention of the state government is to afford protection of the woman for her second delivery, then it should not be based upon the number of children she delivers during those two deliveries.

Sharmila won maternity leave with full pay.

Recently, in January 2018, the central government came forward to give maternity leave to mothers who adopt babies and mothers who get babies by surrogacy. There is also a scheme to give leave to the fathers to help during delivery and child care. In September 2016, Tamil Nadu's AIADMK government led by Jayalalithaa enhanced maternity leave from six to nine months.

References:

i) *Karpagam vs. The Commissioner, Social Welfare and Nutritious Meal Programme, Chennai-5*, W.P. (MD) 10503 of 2005, dt. 18.9.2008

ii) *N. Md. Mohideen & another vs. The Dy. Commissioner of Labour, Chennai & Ors.*, 2008 (5) MLJ 6 (MAD) = 2008 (3) LLJ 362

iii) *J. Sharmila vs. Secretary to Govt., Education Dept. & Anr.*, W.P. (MD) 13555 of 2009, dt. 19.10.2010

On sexual violence

Pothumbu girls

When the first prime minister of India, Pandit Jawaharlal Nehru, was asked which of his government's achievements he considered the foremost, he replied that it was women's education. He was one of the national leaders who believed that India would progress only if women were educated. We now see many women in educational institutions, and in fact the women perform much better than men.

Given these facts, it shocked everyone when, in 2011, the villagers of Pothumbu near Madurai, Tamil Nadu, said that they would not send their girl children to school anymore. The reason was even more shocking. It was because of the bestial conduct of the headmaster of the Pothumbu Government High School. Over his three years at the school, he had sexually abused more than a hundred girls in his care. When the little girls began to share their horror stories with parents, the entire village shuddered. They staged a protest.

On receiving the information, Ms. Brinda Karat, the president of All-India Democratic Women's Association, conducted a direct enquiry and found that the complaints were true. Ponnuthai, the district secretary of AIDWA in the Madurai Rural District, and the parents of the affected students lodged a complaint in the police station, but to no effect. A relative of the headmaster was a teacher at the same school. Other relatives were teachers in nearby schools. They threatened the complainants and verbally abused the affected students. A fact-finding committee headed by U. Nirmala Rani, a Madurai-based advocate, went to the village next. Some of the students had completed their school education by then. Some had even got married. And some were afraid that if they gave evidence, they might face problems. The fact-finding committee tried its best and conducted an inquiry among the students, parents and teachers. It was this committee's report that first brought to light the full extent of the horrors committed by the headmaster. It listed the sexual harassment and violence inflicted by him. He would ask sick students to come to his room and, telling them he was going to pray for their recovery, he would touch their breasts as if marking them with the sign of the cross. He would call students in private and hug them. Under the excuse of looking for something he would insert his hand under their clothes. He also forced some of the children to hold his penis. He would ask the younger girls to sit on his lap, and do unspeakable things to them. Getting students to sweep the floor, he took pictures of them bent over. It is sickening to list these horrible acts.

Veerasamy, father of one of the affected girls, filed a case with the Madurai bench of Madras High Court. He requested that a special investigating team be constituted to investigate this history of sexual abuse and award compensation to his daughter. AIDWA impleaded itself in this petition. As a first step the court directed the involvement of the Child Welfare Committee, under the Protection of Child Rights Act, and directed this committee to file a report. The Child Welfare Committee's report corroborated the charges filed by the fact-finding committee headed by U. Nirmala Rani. The High court was not happy when it examined the records submitted by the police department in respect of the inquiry conducted by them.

It ordered the Madurai district police superintendent to appear in person. Accordingly, Mr. Asra Garg, the superintendent of police, appeared in court. In the meantime, the education department temporarily suspended the headmaster. The police arrested him. Since nobody opposed the grant of bail strongly, he was let out. A relative and a friend who had assisted him were transferred to far-off schools.

The High Court found that a number of the abused children belonged to the SC (Scheduled Castes) community. It ordered that the matter be registered under the SC & ST (Prevention of Atrocities) Act, 1989. Further, that a woman officer of the rank of assistant superintendent should be appointed, that the government appoint a woman special public prosecutor, and an inquiry be conducted under the direct supervision of the district police superintendent. The court stated:

> In this case, admittedly, [a] number of school children [who] belonged to SC community were sexually exploited by the headmaster of the school. Admittedly, the complaints of the children and their parents, if proved, would attract Section 3(1)(xi) and (xii) of the SC and ST (Prevention of Atrocities) Act, 1989. Therefore, in such circumstances, the investigation can be done by an officer not below the rank of Deputy Superintendent of Police. ... In this case, it should be done by a woman police officer who is not below the rank of the Deputy Superintendent of Police.

The High Court ordered that protection be given to the affected girls and care taken that they should not feel threatened when their statements were recorded. The court directed that the girls be given counselling and, whether they were SC or non-SC, the district collector should offer them a compensation of Rs. 1,20,000 each, without waiting for the end of the trial. As soon as the case is registered, the special court should take into account the nature of the case and conclude it expeditiously. The recording of evidence with the girls must be done with sensitivity, the accused teachers must be transferred to far-off schools and on no account should they return to the Pothumbu school.

The court recorded the widespread child sexual abuse and that steps should be taken to remove it. It also stated that:

> [T]he District Collector, Madurai is hereby directed to identify the number of girls from out of the three reports, i.e. fact finding team report headed by Ms. U. Nirmal [*sic*] Rani, . . . report given by the Child Welfare Committee . . . and statements given by the children and their parents to the then Investigating Officer and prepare the [initial] report of those names.

Even after the judgment the inquiry continued; the twenty-four students who complained were given Rs. 28,80,000 as compensation in the first stage. Yet, many students feared the stigma that would be attached to them if they were identified, and did not come forward to make a complaint. The court ordered:

> There may be other children who have not come forward to make a complaint. In such a case, if any complaint is made directly to the District Collector, even those complaints can be entertained by him to award compensation after finding the veracity of the complaints and if there is any prima facie case, not only should the District Collector grant compensation, but also refer those complaints for further investigation by the Investigating Officer.

The High Court directed that if students came forward to complain even at a later date, they should be given compensation after verification. The government paid a total of Rs. 66 lakhs as compensation. Since the judgment, the Pothumbu Government High School has returned to normalcy. The girls now go there to study. Nehru's dream must come true.

Reference:

M. Veerasamy vs. State of Tamil Nadu, 2012 (3) CTC 641

'Vishaka' paved the way

I asked some people, 'Who is Vishaka?' One said she was the daughter of the person living three doors away. Another said they only knew of the temple festival Vaikasi Visakam. But the Vishaka that I am speaking about is an NGO.

Vishaka, along with some other social activists and outfits, filed a case before the Supreme Court. The background of the case was this: in a village of Rajasthan, a social service worker had been subjected to a brutal gang rape in 1992. This PIL was filed on the grounds that it was not enough to take criminal action against the guilty persons. It was also necessary that sufficient protection be given to women in the workplace. The case was heard by a bench headed by the Chief Justice, J.S. Verma. (Justice Verma later headed the committee that was formed by the union government after the Delhi gang rape of 16 December 2012 and gave a detailed report. He passed away in April 2013.) The sad fact is not only that women did not have sufficient protection in the workplace, if a criminal offence was committed against them, they could only approach the police. If they were sexually harassed by their superiors or colleagues there was no dedicated and precise law to protect them and hold the predators to account. Further, there were no rules to take disciplinary action and initiate departmental proceedings. It was also not clear what the term 'sexual harassment' meant.

With its 1997 judgment in *Vishaka vs. State of Rajasthan* the Supreme Court filled the lacuna in the law regarding these issues.

The Supreme Court gave a historic judgment stating that until Parliament enacts a proper law to prevent sexual harassment in the workplace, this judgment would operate as law and it would apply not only to government and public undertakings but also to private organizations. The court declared that men and women were equal in law and that even international conventions stated that there shall be no discrimination against women. It also pointed to the fundamental duties declared in the Constitution, which prohibit practices derogatory to a woman's dignity. The Supreme Court defined sexual harassment as unwelcome sexually determined behaviour, physical contact and verbal and non-verbal contact of a sexual nature, sexually coloured remarks, showing pornography, and other unwelcome conduct of a sexual nature. It also stated that every employer should form a committee to look into the complaints of sexual harassment made by a woman. This committee should consist of a majority of women members and also include a woman representative of an NGO. The Supreme Court further said that disciplinary proceedings should be initiated based on the report given by this committee.

Though this judgment was given in 1997, Parliament enacted the new law only in 2013. In Tamil Nadu, government departments, public sector undertakings and private companies behaved as if they had never heard of the Vishaka judgment. We shall now see how the High Court approached the complaints of women subjected to sexual harassment. The names of these women are not mentioned because they continue to be in service. In 2004, a woman worker in the district electricity board, Theni, made a complaint of sexual harassment against the accounts superintendent. The woman officer who looked into the complaint concluded that it had been proved and therefore recommended that further action should be taken. On the basis of the recommendation the officer was transferred. A departmental inquiry was conducted. The officer challenged the disciplinary proceedings. But the High Court dismissed his writ petition, directing the electricity board to bring its conduct rules in accordance with the Vishaka judgment. The High Court[i] also held that once a woman who was subjected to sexual harassment had given evidence before the complaints committee it was not necessary for her to give evidence again in the departmental inquiry.

A woman who worked as a junior-grade assistant in the state transport department, Coimbatore, complained in 1996 that a colleague had slapped her in public, calling her a prostitute. After due investigation, he was dismissed. Thereafter the department agreed to employ him afresh because of his persistence, but at the starting level, as a junior clerk. He went to the labour court against this. The labour court, ignoring the Vishaka judgment, found his punishment disproportionate and ordered that he be reinstated, with the loss of a year's back wages as penalty for his misbehaviour. The department challenged this before the High Court. The High Court set aside the order of the labour court and also reprimanded it for acting contrary to the principles of the Vishaka judgment.[ii] Its order says, the award of the labour court calls for interference as the labour court had 'in a light-hearted fashion granted the relief without even any discussion on the nature of misconduct committed by the second respondent. Therefore the writ petition stands allowed and the impugned award of the Labour Court is set aside'.

In Trichy, a junior-grade assistant employed via compassionate appointment—since her father had died and she supported a mother and three siblings—complained in 1996 that the fire department supervisor was constantly asking her to accompany him to the movies and that he asked her to come to his room after office hours. The department, which had not formed a Vishaka committee to conduct a proper inquiry, initiated disciplinary proceedings against the woman complainant and ordered a deduction of one year's wages from her.

This was challenged before the High Court and the Court severely reprimanded the department for not conducting a proper inquiry, set aside the order, and directed the department to look into the complaint by forming a Vishaka Committee.[iii] The court noted: 'It is a classic case where the complainant has become the accused and the accused became the complainants.'

The court drew on the case of the *Apparel Export Promotion Council vs. A.K. Chopra* (1999) which stated that '[t]he message of international instruments such as the Convention on the Elimination of All Forms of Discrimination Against Women (CEDAW), 1979, and the Beijing Declaration which directs all State parties to take appropriate measures to prevent discrimination of all forms against women besides taking steps to protect the honour and dignity of women is loud and clear'. Taking these into account, the court ordered:

> [T]he complaint given by the petitioner cannot be lightly brushed aside as done by the respondents. Therefore, the respondents are hereby directed to constitute a committee in the light of the Vishaka case ... Since the respondents have perverted the procedure by making out the petitioner complainant as an accused, the punishment order given to the petitioner ... will stand set aside

A woman who worked as a typist in the Cuddalore labour department complained that a colleague was behaving in an improper manner and abusing her sexually in public. The authorities did not form a Vishaka committee to enquire into this. Instead, in 1999, they held a departmental inquiry against the complainant, set aside her annual increment and also transferred her out of Cuddalore on the grounds that she was causing problems. She challenged the decision before the High Court. The High Court questioned the labour department which instead of taking action against private organizations for not following the Vishaka case, had proceeded in total violation of the Vishaka principles. The court added:

> [W]hen there is complaint and counter complaint and when the counter complaint raises the issue of sexual harassment, it is the bounden duty of the respondents to conduct an enquiry as per the guidelines issued by the Supreme Court in Vishaka's case. It is not open to them to say that her complaint was an afterthought or that it was a counter blast to the [earlier] complaint.

The High Court set aside the punishment and directed an inquiry against the male worker, according to the Vishaka Case.[iv]

What happened in a private company in Hosur was strange. A woman employee had to reach home urgently and asked for a lift from a male employee. Misusing this opportunity, the man behaved to her in an improper manner even as he was driving his scooter. He was an important figure in the labour union. The employer looked into her complaint and initiated disciplinary proceedings against the male employee. On proof of guilt he was removed from service. At that, he went to the labour court. The labour court, without appreciating the evidence properly, ordered his reinstatement with back wages. The management went to the High Court. The male employee argued that the management was acting in bad faith against him because of his union activities and that the complainant was a mere puppet in their hands. But the High Court, taking into account the clear evidence of the woman complainant during the departmental inquiry, set aside the labour court's award.[v] The court also highlighted:

> This Court do [*sic*] not appreciate the stand of the Labour Court, and the award of the Labour Court is liable to be interfered with. There is no necessity to interfere with the quantum of punishment, when the evidence placed against the workman was completely justified and the findings of the misconduct and also the proportionality of punishment, does not call for any interference.

The Erode electricity board ordered an inquiry against a woman employee contending that her complaint of sexual harassment against certain officers was false. The Madras High Court said in *V. Govindaraj vs. The Superintendent Engineer, Tamil Nadu Electricity Distribution Circle, Theni, and Ors.* (2007) that if action is taken against the complainant, it would discourage women from making complaints and that such action violates the rights of the women employees. The Court set aside the complaint made by the department against the woman.

You can see that various kinds of cases keep coming to the High Court on the basis of the Vishaka judgment. If you examine the cases above you will see that in a majority of them, the woman makes a complaint of sexual harassment and all the other employees gang up on her, making her out to be the guilty party.

In 2013, the new law—Sexual Harassment of Women at Workplace (Prevention, Prohibition and Redressal) Act, 2013—enacted by Parliament brought in some changes. There is provision for appeal before a tribunal against the decision of the complaints committee. There are also provisions for complainants to arrive at a compromise, and provisions for taking action against persons who make false complaints. Under this new law it is not only employees who can make a complaint; the law also applies to women who are under contract employment and who come to a workplace seeking employment. It is welcome news that this law has enlarged the scope of the Vishaka judgment and has also given a warning to false complainants.

References:

i) *V. Govindaraj vs. The Superintendent Engineer, Tamil Nadu Electricity Distribution Circle, Theni, and Ors.*, W.P. (MD) No. 4638 of 2004, dt. 26.07.2007

ii) *The Management of Tamil Nadu State Transport Corporation vs. The Presiding Officer, Labour Court, Salem*, W.P. No. 15588 of 1998, dt. 27.1.2009

iii) *S. Chitra vs. The Director of Fire Services*, W.P. No. 37598 of 2006, dt. 30.09.2009

iv) *Smt. V. Barani vs. Inspector of Labour*, W.P. Nos. 6755 and 6756 of 2007, dt. 05.04.2010

v) *The Management of Hirsch Watch Straps (P) Ltd., Hosur vs. The Presiding Officer, Labour Court, Salem*, W.P. No. 37091 of 2003, dt. 07.06.2011

The dying declaration that came alive

Every year at the Koovagam festival we see the sad ritual of transwomen (the aravanis) removing their thalis—the thread or chain worn around the neck, signifying a woman's marriage—before the deity Aravan and mourning his death as widows. We will now see the story of an aravani's death, and the cruelty that the trans-community faces.

Pandian worked as an assistant in a vegetable shop in Vyasarpadi, Chennai district. He had a friend called Saranraj. On 1 May 2006 the police came to Pandian's home, claiming to be in search of Saranraj in connection with a theft. They took Pandian to the police station for interrogation, telling his family that he would be returned once they had Saranraj's whereabouts. While he remained in their custody, he was produced before the Egmore magistrate court for four days. Since he was shown as an accused in a theft case, the court remanded him in custody for a further fifteen days and sent him to the Chennai central jail. It was here that the tragedy of Pandian the aravani began.

Almost as soon as he entered prison some of the prisoners began to subject Pandian to extreme sexual violence. They sodomized him repeatedly for days while Pandian screamed in pain. He begged his sister Jayalakshmi, who came to visit him in prison, to get him out on bail regardless of the expense. On hearing of the violence suffered by her brother (or sister, as Pandian self-identified) who was not yet eighteen years old, Jayalakshmi borrowed a large amount of money and gave it to the advocate; bail was granted on 19 May 2006. The magistrate released Pandian on condition that he report at the Vyasarpadi police station every day at 10 AM and sign his presence in a register. Now began the second chapter of Pandian's torture. Having suffered sexual violence in jail for fifteen days he suffered a repeat of the same violence at the hands of the policemen at Vyasarpadi Police Station. A police constable would pick up Pandian every morning at 8 AM. He was kept at the police station till 11 in the night and raped brutally. When his mother saw that Pandian returned late and totally exhausted from the police station she wanted to know why, but he turned her away. He opened up to his sister Jayalakshmi and told her what he was being put through day after day. When his mother went to the police station to make a complaint, she was beaten up.

Unable to bear the sexual violence Pandian did not go to the police station for two days. However, the policemen forced him to come back, threatening to get his bail cancelled and send him back to jail. Unable to decide between the two hells facing him, Pandian decided to kill himself. On 12 June 2006 he brought some kerosene, went to the police station, poured it over himself and set it alight. He was admitted with thirty-five per cent burns in the Stanley Hospital. Then he was sent to the burns department of Kilpauk Hospital. Not content with torturing him, the police filed a second case against him, this time with the charge of attempted suicide. They went to the hospital and tried getting Pandian to sign blank sheets before they were chased out by the medical staff. After seventeen days in treatment, Pandian died on 29 June 2006. As he was dying, the XXIII Metropolitan Magistrate recorded Pandian's dying declaration at the request of the medical officer. The court cited:

> [T]he dying declaration recorded by the Metropolitan Magistrate, who was examined as Witness No. 23, clearly shows that the said Pandian has given statement before the Magistrate to the effect that for the past one month he was harassed by the police. It is also seen that in the dying declaration, he has stated that the police threatened him that a false case would be foisted against him and [they] also heckled at him ... and it was due to that reason he has committed suicide by dousing himself in kerosene and setting it afire.

Normally a statement given by a person at the point of death is accepted to be true since no one would lie at that moment. The Indian Evidence Act regards such a declaration as admissible evidence. Now we will see how Pandian's statement was important. No one came forward to give evidence regarding the sexual violence inflicted on Pandian or his attempt to set fire to himself. No one stepped forward to speak the truth. In November 2006, Jayalakshmi filed a case seeking compensation for Pandian's death and initiating action against the constables Kumar, Ravi, Sampath, inspectors Chinna Pandian, Thirunavukarasu and station writer Rajendran. The division bench admitted the petition and asked the State to file its counter. On 10 November 2006 a journal called *Naveena Netrikkan* published a story on the violence inflicted on Pandian at the police station, due to his being a transgender person. Since the paper stated that the police department was trying to suppress the dying declaration, the High Court directed the editor to file the details known to him. The charge of wilful suppression was denied by the police department which stated that no such incident had happened. Since contradictory versions were filed, the High Court ordered an inquiry by a district judge. The High Court Registrar (Vigilance) Selvi Mala (who later became a Judge of Madras High Court) was appointed as the inquiry officer. After recording the evidence of forty-six witnesses, she filed her report on 16 February 2007. The report stated that Pandian had killed himself within the police precincts because of the sexual violence inflicted by the policemen. After due inquiry the High Court delivered its judgment on 10 July 2007. It held that the sexual violence was proved. The court noted:

> [T]here is abundant evidence to show that the respondents 4 to 8 have in fact committed drastic inhuman violence on the body of the petitioner's brother Pandian, which is not only a human right violation, but also not expected of the police personnel like respondents 4 to 8, who are to safeguard the interest of the public.

It directed the government to initiate a departmental inquiry against the five policemen, awarded Rs. 5 lakhs as compensation to the family of the deceased Pandian. The compensation was to be paid by the state government. The Court left it open to the State to deduct the amount from the salaries of the policemen. It was the dying declaration recorded by the magistrate that greatly helped to prove the case. The legal proceedings started on 18 November concluded eight months later in July 2007. The High Court has to be congratulated for this. The judgment quoted from two significant Supreme Court judgments.

1) *Rudul Sah vs. State of Bihar* (1983):

> The defence of sovereign immunity being inapplicable, and alien to the concept of guarantee of fundamental rights, there can be no question of such a defence being available in the constitutional remedy.

This was to deal with the principle of sovereign immunity claimed as defence by government servants in respect of an act committed by them in the course of their work.

2) *Munshi Singh Gautam (dead) and others vs. State of Madhya Pradesh* (2005):

> The courts must not lose sight of the fact that death in police custody is perhaps one of the worst kinds of crime in a civilised society governed by the rule of law, and poses a serious threat to an orderly civilised society. Torture in custody flouts the basic rights of the citizens recognised by the Indian Constitution and is an affront to human dignity.

The hospital workers and doctors, who acted with alertness and integrity to foil the policemen who attempted to undermine the case, must be applauded. At this time when the State has taken steps to rehabilitate aravanis who have undergone sex change operations, our society must think of the sexual violence they suffer. This suffering is echoed year after year by the crowd that gathers in Koovagam.

Reference:

Jayalakshmi vs. State of Tamil Nadu, 2007 (2) MLJ (Crl.) 453 Mad. = 2007 (4) MLJ 849

On religiosity and the right to practise religion

Pinnaiyakkal

There are male and female deities. But is there any mandate that only male priests should offer worship to the deities?

Shall we look at the story of Pinnaiyakkal who fought for this right to conduct worship, in the process antagonizing her family, her people and the whole village?

Nalludevanpatti is a tiny village in Usilampatti taluk of Madurai district, Tamil Nadu. Pinna Thevar was the priest of the Durga Devi temple. The temple had been in the care of his family for generations. In 2004, the priest Pinna Thevar told his only child Pinnaiyakkal that it was now her responsibility to offer pooja at the temple. Right from childhood she had been with her father when he performed the pooja, and had learnt the rites and rituals well. The problem started after her father died in November 2006. Pinna Thevar's brother Gurunathan's sons insisted that only a man could be the next priest and that the position belonged to them, as Pinna Thevar's male descendants. They confronted Pinnaiyakkal saying that she had no right to be the temple-priest. Pinnaiyakkal filed a case in the Usilampatti Munsif Court.

Even as the civil dispute was pending, the whole village turned into a battlefield over the question of a woman's right to perform as a priest. The situation turned so bad that the tahsildar of Usilampatti had to intervene. There was a village meeting presided over by the Village Lords. The conclusion was 'eighty-nine per cent of the villagers have agreed that Pinnaiyakkal's cousin shall be the priest. This is the consensus arrived at by the representatives of the Puththur Naalukaraivagaraia, the village people living in the three municipalities of Vadugapatti, Nalludevanpatti and Pothampatti.'

The revenue authorities have the power to interfere if there is any danger to public peace and order. The Criminal Procedure Code recognizes the tahsildar, revenue divisional officer and the district collector as executive magistrates. After restoring law and order they should advise the person or group disturbing the peace to approach the civil courts for remedy. They are empowered to order the maintenance of status quo till then.

The tahsildar of Usilampatti, a woman, went to Nalludevanpatti village to restore the peace. But she did something very strange. She accepted the decision of the villagers, took away the right to do pooja from Pinnaiyakkal and gave it to her cousin. Pinnaiyakkal walked out of the meeting and filed a case challenging the biased order.

The court pointed out several errors in the tahsildar's order and said that her exercise of power was not in accordance with law. The court noted:

> Even assuming such a meeting was convened by the powers vested ... under the Criminal Procedure Code (CrPC), by which the tahsildar was empowered to be an executive magistrate, but in the guise of exercising such magisterial powers under CrPC, the third respondent (tahsildar) cannot override the rights of parties. No provisions of the CrPC authorises the executive magistrate to make such decision as had been made in the present case.

She should have directed the parties to resolve their dispute in the civil court, until which time Pinnaiyakkal should have been allowed to continue as priest and perform pooja.

The tahsildar who had issued the erroneous order contended that Pinnaiyakkal could not be the priest. The High Court addressed the question of whether a woman can be a priest:

> Even in Vedic times it is recorded that women had performed poojas and rituals. Fortunately the present temple is not trapped under any agama sastras. The sub-cultural deities established in the Southern parts of India are freed from the norms of Manu Smritis and hence the women being subordinated to home making alone was not warranted. As said by a great philosopher the women hold half the sky and for the human progress we must walk with our two legs. The altars of the God must be made free from gender bias. Only then the constitutional mandate under Articles 15 and 51-A(e) will become a reality.

The Court stressed that if the country is to progress, both men and women must step forward together. The altar of God must be free from gender bias. The Court invoked Article 15 of the Constitution that bars discrimination against women, and Article 51-A(e) which makes it a fundamental duty to abjure practices derogatory to women.

The Court set aside the order of the tahsildar and ordered that the district collector and the police must enforce its decision. The police went in full force and handed over the keys of the Durgai Amman temple to Pinnaiyakkal.

But the sequel to the case is tragic. Though Pinnaiyakkal won the civil suit in the Usilampatti court and her right was upheld, the tenacious cousins filed appeals against the verdict and have prevented her from doing pooja to date. The district administration is in deep, uncaring slumber.

The temple in question is not constructed according to the Agamas, the orthodox scriptural tradition. Recently, in December 2015, the Supreme Court has ordered in a case filed by Sivacharyas that in the temples in Tamil Nadu that are Agamic, only a particular community is entitled to function as priests. It is disappointing that the Court did not say that women of that community can be priests, too. Moreover it is rank patriarchy to hold that women cannot even visit certain temples. In September 2018, the Supreme Court declared as invalid the bar on women between the ages five and fifty visiting Sabarimalai. In April 2016, the Shani temple at Shingnapur, Maharashtra, was opened to women worshippers, despite opposition.

Women's right to equality still exists only on paper, the realization of this right is light years away.

Reference:

Pinnaiyakkal vs. The District Collector, Madurai District, 2008 (3) TLNJ 640 (civil)

Muhabath Beevi

Long debates are conducted today regarding crimes and the award of punishment. The question of what is the appropriate punishment for any offence has become a matter of discussion among the public and in the press and visual media. The Indian Penal Code lays down the maximum punishment that may be awarded for each offence. Once the offence is proved and before the award of punishment, the court questions the accused, takes into account extenuating circumstances and considers whether there are any reasons to reduce the sentence. The guilty person may challenge the verdict by way of an appeal before the High Court or the Supreme Court, arguing that the punishment is excessive. In the same way the complainant or the State may also appeal against a sentence on the grounds that it is not adequate. The appellate court has the jurisdiction to give a decision and award appropriate punishment. In certain extraordinary criminal cases, the appellate court is even empowered by law to enhance the punishment on its own. But there is no provision to ascertain that the punishment makes amends to the victim or affords them satisfaction. In many countries, the victims or the families of victims have the right to be asked what is the appropriate sentence for the person convicted. By a recent amendment which came into force on 26 January 2016, under the terms of the Prevention of Atrocities Act, victims have the right to oppose bail to the accused and their lawyer may take part in the inquiry, giving their opinion on the sentence to be awarded. Under this legislation, not only the accused but also the victims are provided with procedural guarantees.

A strange case came before the High Court where the victim's opinion was sought regarding punishment. On 23 September 2007 Muhabath Beevi, a Muslim woman from Ramanathapuram, was arrested during the Iddath period—which typically lasts three to four lunar months—after she had lost her husband. The police station house officer, Inspector Vasantha, along with ten women constables, entered Muhabath Beevi's house at 4.30 AM in the morning and arrested her. She was wearing a lungi at the time and was not even permitted to change her clothes or observe the pre-dawn rituals of the Ramzan fast. At the Ramanathapuram Police Station, she was not allowed to get in touch with her family. Though she complained of chest pain, no arrangement was made to give her medical aid till late in the evening. She had been arrested on the basis of a dowry harassment complaint made by her daughter-in-law, but was not informed of the reasons for her arrest. The Constitution gives protection to a person arrested or detained and recognizes certain rights. In the case of *D.K. Basu vs. State of West Bengal* (1996) the Supreme Court laid down eleven guidelines for the police in case of arrest or detention. These include the memo of arrest, to be countersigned by the arrestee and an independent witness (relation or neighbour) at the time of arrest. Further, news of the arrest must be conveyed 'as soon as practicable' to a trusted relative or acquaintance of the arrestee, and the person under arrest is to be informed of this right at once. The arrested person must be medically examined by a trained doctor every forty-eight hours. The Supreme Court also said that if any police officer violates these guidelines, they could be punished for contempt of court.

The counsel for Muhabath Beevi filed a contempt petition against Inspector Vasantha for violating the D.K. Basu guidelines.

The Madurai bench of the Madras High Court ordered the inspector to appear in person and give her explanation. On examining her explanation and the police records the court found that Inspector Vasantha had violated two of the D.K. Basu guidelines: Muhabath Beevi was not informed of the grounds of arrest or allowed to contact a relation, friend or advocate; the mandatory diary entry of the arrest should have been made immediately, but it was not. Vasantha had also fabricated the information presented to the Court. The arrest memo given to Muhabath Beevi's brother showed the time of arrest as 11.30 AM and the place of arrest was given as the bus stand. The bench concluded that the police did not give medical aid (as mandated by the D.K. Basu guidelines) and also did not properly inform her family. It stated:

> The counter affidavit filed by the respondent is only an attempt to cover up the violations of D.K. Basu guidelines. Though the respondent claims that the petitioner was arrested at 11.30 PM near the bus stand, it is only a fabrication of the records. As can be seen from the supporting affidavit, the arrest was made around 4.30 AM in the house of the petitioner. There is no reason as to why the petitioner should be found loitering near the bus stand around 11.30 AM at the time of her arrest as suggested by the respondent.

The law provides that if contempt is proved the contemnor can be awarded six months' imprisonment and a fine of Rs. 2,000. The Tamil Nadu Subordinate Police Officers' Conduct Rules, 1964, state that a government servant may be removed from service if found guilty of contempt.

The Court felt that punitive action against the inspector would not afford relief to Muhabath Beevi. This Muslim widow, who was observing the Ramzan fast, was arrested at an unearthly hour and dragged out in front of the public; she had suffered great humiliation. The loss of dignity she had suffered could not be compensated with any amount of money. At the same time if the inspector was punished, she would lose her job. So the Court considered what punishment should be awarded to the inspector which would make amends for the wrong done to Muhabath Beevi.

The court referred to an observation made by the Supreme Court in the D.K. Basu case (cited above). In paragraph 55, it observed:

> The objective is to apply balm to the wounds and not to punish the transgressor or the offender, as awarding appropriate punishment for the offence (irrespective of compensation) must be left to the Criminal Courts in which the offender is prosecuted, which the State, in law, is duty bound to do.

The court said that if Inspector Vasantha wanted to avoid being punished, she should go to Muhabath Beevi's house and offer a public apology. If Muhabath Beevi accepted the apology, the Court would reconsider the question of punishment.

> [I]t was entirely for the respondent (Inspector Vasantha) to take this course of action and any decision in this regard is purely voluntary. When this suggestion was made by this Court on 19.09.2008, the respondent who was also present readily agreed to go to the house of the petitioner (Muhabath Beevi) and assuage her hurt feelings by tendering apology to her in person.

After some initial hesitation, the inspector went to Muhabath

Beevi's house and asked for forgiveness, in public. This was covered in headlines by all the newspapers of the district. This was the first time an errant police officer had publicly sought forgiveness from the victim.

The counsel for Muhabath informed the Court that his client had accepted the apology. The Court then warned the inspector that she must not repeat such acts in future and closed the case. This case showed the importance of restoring dignity to the victim and of making it a judicial priority.

Reference:

Muhabath Beevi vs. Mrs. Vasantha, Contempt Petition No. 16 of 2008, dt. 26.9.2008

Jane Sathya/Queen Sheeba

The former Chief Justice of India, Altamas Kabir went to the law college in Kashmir University as a chief guest. After his speech was over, as per custom the National Anthem was played. Some law college students remained seated at that time without showing respect to the National Anthem. It saddened others to see law students behave like this directly after being addressed by the Chief Justice. In 1962, after the Indo-China conflict, a decision was taken that the National Anthem would be played in all cinema halls in Tamil Nadu, at the end of the movie. It was intended to boost patriotism. But what happened in reality was different. The audience started leaving the hall even before the last scene. Seeing this, the order was withdrawn.

I am reminded of an incident that happened in Kerala in 1985. As per a circular of the education department, the National Anthem must be sung at school every day during the morning assembly. One morning when the National Anthem was being sung, three children—Bijoe, Binu Mol, and Bindu Emmanuel—stood up with the rest, but they did not sing the Anthem. This was seen by a news reporter who informed an MLA. The issue was raised in the Kerala Legislative Assembly. A committee was formed to inquire into the incident. The three students appeared before the committee and said that they belonged to the group of Christians called Jehovah's Witnesses. As per their belief they must praise only God and not a race, a language or rivers. They said that they have never disrespected the flag. On the basis of the inquiry committee report, the deputy inspector of schools expelled the students from school by order (dt. 26 July 1985). The father of the children made several representations. But he obtained no relief. Then the children approached the Kerala High Court but here too their petition was dismissed. So they went to the Supreme Court.

The decision (1986) of the bench consisting of Justice Chinnappa Reddy (who died in April 2013) is a historic one. The Supreme Court said that Indian citizens have the right to follow the religion of their choice and there can be no interference with religious beliefs. Though the students did not sing the anthem along with the others, they did not disrespect the anthem and they were standing in the assembly. The Supreme Court also stressed that while religious rights have to be protected disrespecting national symbols cannot be permitted. The court noted:

> We are satisfied, in the present case, that the expulsion of the three children from the school for the reason that because of their conscientiously held religious faith, they do not join the singing of the National Anthem in the morning assembly, though they do stand up respectfully when the anthem is sung, is a violation of their fundamental right to 'freedom of conscience and freely to profess, practise and propagate religion'. (Para 25 in *Bijoe Emmanuel and others vs. State of Kerala*)

It must be remembered that the act of the students in Kashmir who did not conduct themselves with respect to the National Anthem would not be protected by this judgment.

While addressing a PIL on 25 July 2017, the Madras High Court under Justice M.V. Muralidharan's direction has ordered that the National Anthem should be sung in the morning at every school. It is not clear on what basis this order was passed. There are many cases where religious rights and educational institutions have run up against each other. Let us look at some of them. Jane Sathya[i] was a student at the Meenakshi Sundaram Engineering College. She was a Christian belonging to the Seventh Day Adventist Church. Her father was the principal of a school run by the sect. Seventh Day Adventists do not work on Saturdays, instead they engage in religious activities. Just as Sunday is a sacred day for other Christians, for this group it is Saturday. This creed was founded in America in the nineteenth century and it declared that Sabbath should be observed from Friday sunset to Saturday sunset. A shock awaited Jane Sathya after she had paid her fees at the engineering college. She learnt that the college worked on Saturdays. Immediately she wrote a letter that she must be granted leave on Saturdays. The administration replied that Saturday was a working day and she could not be given special privilege for non-attendance. She asked for a transfer certificate and went to another college. But she filed a case before the High Court that the college should refund the admission fees she had paid and that she had a right to protection of her religion, citing the Bijoe Emmanuel case. The High Court dismissed her petition, holding that the above decision would not apply to Jane Sathya: the college syllabus and time-table cannot be altered to suit the religious observances of a single student. The court noted:

> The first respondent college running classes on Saturdays cannot be said to be either depriving the petitioner's right to have her religious faith, nor has she a right to absent herself on a day which is prescribed as a working day of the college. The calendar had been fixed for all students concerned. Hence

> there is no case made out by the petitioner. Accordingly, the writ petition will stand dismissed.

Many educational institutions have been founded by Christian organizations. Though many of them receive government grants, the government cannot interfere in the administration in view of Article 30 of the Constitution which protects minority rights. It is the right of the minority institutions to decide whom they appoint. The education department can only fix the educational and age criteria for such posts. Registration in employment exchange and the reservation policy do not apply to these institutions. Every Christian institution will have its own rules for the appointment of teachers. They prepare a list of qualified Christian teachers in their own parishes and make appointments according to these. Even if they violate a rule no one can challenge it in court. In 2010, Queen Sheeba[ii] from Ambur filed a case that though there was a post of physical instructor in a school run by the religious minority to which she belonged, she was not given the appointment which went to a person belonging to the Hindu faith. The High Court which heard her case dismissed it. It said that the courts cannot interfere in a school run by Christians, as it is a minority school; there is no bar against appointing a Hindu teacher and in fact the administration should be commended for appointing a person of another faith. It said:

> Even in respect of a Christian minority school, since the right to manage the school is vested with the management, it is open to them to appoint any candidate, who has the necessary qualifications. The Supreme Court has held that if a minority institution acts like a secular institution, that can be welcomed. There is no bar to a minority institution admitting even a

non minority student in the school or appointing teachers belonging to other religions for teaching their candidates. … In the absence of any legal or enforceable right on the part of the petitioner, this court is not inclined to entertain the writ petition.

The history of cases involving religious rights and educational institutions is like a prolonged soap opera.

References:

i) *Jane Sathya vs. Meenakshi Sundaram Engineering College*, W.P. No. 19215 of 2008, dt.17.7.2012

ii) *W. Queen Sheeba vs. Joint Director of School Education, Chennai*, 2010 (3) MLJ 917 = 2010 (2) CWC 126

Right to life, choice and dignity: Mapping personal journeys

Pothumallee

In the mid-1920s, there was a huge conflict within the Congress party over the manner in which food was served on the basis of caste at the Tamil Gurukula School run by V.V.S. Aiyar in Cheranmadevi, Thirunelveli district. Here, two Brahmin boys were fed in a separate room from other students. On 10 March 1925 Mahatma Gandhi wrote a letter on this subject to Dr. Varadarajulu Naidu:

> With reference to the Gurukul controversy I told Mr. Iyer that I would not give a definite opinion unless I had seen you and heard you. Having heard you, it seems to me that in so far as the present brahmacharis are concerned, if the parents of the brahmin boys insist on their boys being allowed to dine separately, their scruples should be respected. But, for the future, it may be announced that no brahmacharis would be accepted whose parents would not let their boys dine in the same row with the others. I understand from you that the cook at the Gurukul would be always a brahmin. What you object to (and that properly) is the separating of non-brahmin boys from the brahmins. I do think that all the boys should sit in the same row whilst they are taking their meals. (*Collected Works of Mahatma Gandhi*, vol. 30, p. 371)

Although the Gurukulam was a private organization it had

received financial assistance from the Congress party. So E.V. Ramasamy (Periyar), Dr. Varadarajulu Naidu and others severely criticized the caste discrimination practised in serving food at the Gurukulam. The Congress Committee passed a resolution by majority, that if the Gurukulam did not mend its ways, the Congress party would withdraw financial assistance to it. Even after this there was no consensus within the Tamil Nadu Congress Party. Therefore, EVR and Dr. Varadarajulu resigned their membership of the party.

At the time, samapandi bhojanam (inter-caste dining) was undertaken as a social activity to erase caste differences. After India attained independence our Constitution included Article 17 which abolished untouchability. To date, the practice of untouchability has not vanished. Marginalized people continue to live in cheris/slums, they can be stopped and humiliated if they enter town wearing footwear, while the two-tumbler convention is still practised at tea shops. We remember as a prime example of untouchability, the dividing wall that was constructed around 1989–90 in the village of Utthapuram, some forty kilometres from Madurai, between neighbourhoods occupied by the dominant pillai caste and the Dalit mallar communities. The wall stood till 2008, when it was demolished by the Madurai district administration.

Article 47 of the Constitution declares that it is the duty of the State to ensure the health of its citizens by providing them with nutritious food. To date no government has taken any steps in this regard.

When K. Kamarajar was chief minister (1954–62) of Tamil Nadu, noon meals were provided in some schools on a trial basis. The wheat bran, soya, oil and milk powder supplied by the US Government under the PL 480 scheme was used for this. It was not run as a comprehensive scheme. Moreover, in the face of strong opposition from developing countries, USA revised its food aid programme in 1966. Thereafter, when M.G. Ramachandran was chief minister (1977–87), he introduced a noon meal scheme in all schools. Initially, it was introduced by giving financial assistance to village panchayats. Later, the entire scheme was brought under the control of the Social Welfare Department. Noon meal centres were established in every government, corporation, and aided school. Three posts were created at each centre, those of noon meal organizer, cook, and assistant. In the Government Order (GO) issued in 1997, a condition was imposed that the women selected for these posts should live within one kilometre of the village where the centre was located. While nearly one lakh posts were created in noon meal centres throughout Tamil Nadu, no reservation was made for women belonging to the Scheduled Castes. Moreover, because of the one-kilometre rule, Dalit women could not apply for the post. Since Dalit neighbourhoods were outside village limits, these women were excluded from appointment. This iniquity occurred despite the fact that selection to these posts was made by the state government or under its direct supervision, and the centres were funded entirely by the central government, i.e. with public money. Reservation was not provided for SC and ST employees.

The government practised discrimination even in the appointment of the Anganwadi assistants. To justify the non-implementation of reservation, the Tamil Nadu government took advantage of a circular issued by the Central Government in 2003:

> Please refer to your letter No. SSW-473/2003 dated 17.10.2003 on the subject mentioned above. The ICDS Scheme envisages Anganwadi Workers (AWWs) and Helpers to be 'honorary workers' from the local community. Consequently, no

reservation for SCs/STs and OBCs in their selection has been provided under the Scheme as they are not deemed to be 'Government employees'.

In the case of *P. Vasantha vs. The District Collector, Dindigul*—reported in 2007 (6) MLJ 402—the High Court had given a judgment stating that the condition that applicants should live within a one-kilometre radius from the noon meal centre was unconstitutional. The Court said that while priority may be given to applicants who lived in the vicinity of the noon meal centres and Anganwadi centres, this would happen only when two applicants had obtained the same marks in the selection process. Yet, Dalit women did not get justice even after this.

This was when a woman named Pothumallee from Thiruvarur district filed a writ petition. She stated that principles of social justice were not followed in filling the posts in the noon meal centres and that reservation must be implemented while appointing persons to these posts. The High Court which heard this case narrated the earlier incident and controversy at the Tamil Gurukulam of V.V.S. Aiyar, and also the difference of opinion that arose at the time between Mahatma Gandhi and Periyar. Gandhi had conceded that Brahmin cooks may be appointed in order to assuage dominant-caste feelings, insisting only on the point that all students eat together. The Court said that appointing a Dalit woman in accordance with the policy of reservation is not only an act of economic empowerment but it will change the marginalization suffered by Dalits in society. The court therefore noted:

In the existing guidelines framed by the Government for filling up the post of workers under the Nutritious Meal scheme as well as Anganwadi workers, preference is given to residents of the village or to persons who are living with[in] the same locality. In most of the cases, either schools or Anganwadi centres are located in the hamlets dominated by upper castes and applying preference as indicated in the guidelines, will clearly edge out the members of Scheduled Caste from getting opportunity to work in such centres, since hardly there are any schools or Anganwadi centres situated in the Dalit colonies. That was why the Supreme Court also in the Right to Food case gave direction to States to make efforts that all Scheduled Caste and Scheduled Tribe colonies in the Country must have Anganwadi Centres. Such direction may take years to achieve.

The Court said the children who eat the food cooked by a Dalit will learn to reject the untouchability practised in respect of the community. Moreover, the Court draws from *Bharat Sevashram Sangh vs. State of Gujarat*, reported in 1986 (4) SCC 51; the Supreme Court judgment notes:

> The insistence on having teachers belonging to the Scheduled Castes and the Scheduled Tribes is also in the public interest. Children should be brought up in an atmosphere where there is opportunity to mix freely with students and teachers belonging to traditionally disfavoured communities also. The opportunity to show reverence to teachers belonging to the Scheduled Castes and Scheduled Tribes will in the long run enable the child brought up in that atmosphere to shed the feeling of superiority over members belonging to the Scheduled Castes and the Scheduled Tribes. Such an atmosphere would

also be congenial to the development of a society consisting of persons free from feelings of hatred or contempt towards others.

The Court added that the Tamil Nadu Government need not follow the Central Government Circular and that the roster system set out in the GO of 30 June 2008, dividing staff intake by community shares, must be compulsorily adopted while filling the posts in all the noon meal scheme centres in Tamil Nadu. This order was passed on 19 April 2010.

The then chief minister, Kalaignar Karunanidhi, immediately implemented this judgment and issued GO No. 142 (Social Welfare) on 6 July 2010. Pothumallee's fight resulted in the creation of opportunity for nearly 25,000 Dalit women to be appointed by reservation. It is a matter of regret that she, the prime mover, has not got any appointment to date. Following Tamil Nadu's example, the chief minister of Uttar Pradesh, Mayawati, issued a GO which faced stiff resistance from vested interests. According to a report in *India Today* (17 July 2010), over 1,000 children in UP shifted schools, from government-run to private ones, to avoid mid-day meals prepared by Dalit cooks. A study released in March 2009 by the Jan Sahas Social Development Society reveals how untouchability continues to be practised in Madhya Pradesh's schools, where sixty-three per cent of Dalit children reported being made to sit in separate rows from other students for the mid-day meal. But in Tamil Nadu, since there is greater awareness of social justice, the Pothumallee case had a huge impact.

Reference:

D. Pothumallee vs. District Collector, Thiruvarur, 2010 (5) MLJ 46

Tamilarasi

Today, Tamilarasi is not alive to taste the sweetness of her victory. But no one should have to face the humiliation and threats that she did. The battle for justice she fought was a very important one and unprecedented.

Tamilarasi was a post-graduate. She was unmarried. She lived with her aged parents and gave tuition in English to children who lived near her house. She was also an Anganwadi worker, who had joined service in 1982 and completed twenty-five years of work, during which she received an award for outstanding work from the district collector. She was removed from service in 2006 because of a dispute that had arisen between her and her superior. The formal account stated that the district collector of Tuticorin ordered her removal from service. But what happened was a bit more complicated. While she was on medical leave, Thilana Mohanambal, her superior, obtained a certificate from the assistant medical officer to declare Tamilarasi a schizophrenic. The certificate was sent to the district collector. Her removal from service was ordered on the basis of this certificate. As the Court would later note:

> In the present case, neither any enquiry was held nor any reasonable opportunity was given to the petitioner to defend herself. The charge memo followed by dismissal order were all done during the months of January, February of 2006, when

the petitioner was admittedly under medical leave supported by certificates and leave applications.

Tamilarasi filed a writ petition with the Madurai bench of Madras High Court. The Court observed:

> It was rather unfortunate that the third respondent, even though he is Child Development Officer, should choose to . . . state that the petitioner was [of an] insane mental condition. Such words do not find a place in any relevant statutes. Nor did she, being a Welfare officer, make any attempts to find out the petitioner's condition including her family background. She also did not make any attempt to send her to medical board for an appropriate certificate as required under the Mental Health Act, 1987.

The Indian Lunacy Act, 1912, which was in force during colonial times has been scrapped; in 1987 Parliament enacted the Mental Health Act. Under this Act, only a medical committee which includes a psychiatrist can determine who is a mentally-ill person. Though there are different kinds of mental diseases, a mentally-ill person as defined in the Act is a person 'in need of treatment . . . [for] any mental disorder other than mental retardation'. The first problem was to ascertain whether Tamilarasi was really mentally unwell and whether she had schizophrenia. This cannot be done by turning to just any medical officer on hand as her superior, Thilana Mohanambal, had done.

Tamilarasi said in Court that it was wrong to say she was mentally unwell and the order of termination should be set aside. After much thought, she agreed to submit to an investigation by the Madurai Rajaji Hospital. The head of the psychiatric department,

Dr. Ramasubramaniam, kept her under observation for one month and certified that she did not suffer from any mental disease that prevented her from discharging her duties. The report specifies:

> I am of the opinion that she is suffering from Paranoid Schizophrenic illness and all her symptoms are well controlled with drugs and she is in lucid interval. Under the supervision of a mental health professional and effective Antipsychotic drugs and Mood stabilizers, she will be able to carry out her official responsibility.

This certificate was sent in a sealed cover and thereafter the case was listed. Once the government pleader knew the tenor of the certificate, he tried to get the matter adjourned. The Court informed the counsel that the judgment would be delivered on 10 October 2007, an appropriate day in the opinion of the Court as it was World Mental Health Day.

Though a day has been dedicated to foreground mental health issues, we remain unaware of it. We also tend to casually dismiss mental disease as something that occurs in western countries. In any town with 1,00,000 people at least 300 persons would have mental health problems. A common recourse in Tamil Nadu is to take such persons to places like the Ervadi dargah and Gunaseelam Vishnu Temple, both in Ramanathapuram district. At these places mental healthcare and religious ritual are combined for treatment, which is given free of cost. If somebody approaches a psychiatrist, we label them mad. In Kanyakumari, we had an instance where the collector labelled beggars as mentally ill and packed them off to the mental health hospital in Chennai, merely to remove them from the locality.

The Court condemned the termination order which had

been passed without any justification or inquiry and ordered that Tamilarasi should be reinstated with back wages. It stated:

> [In] the case for a Government Servant who develops disability during service it is too late in the day for the respondents to label a person as insane on their own and declare her unfit for a Government employment without any factual material. It makes a rather sad commentary. This only shows the utter ignorance of the respondents in understanding the special legislation occupying the field. This requires a greater sensitisation of the administration.

The district collector who had acted without any sensitivity about mental health was awarded a fine of Rs. 5,000.

If a government servant becomes mentally ill while in service and is unable to discharge her duties, she cannot be summarily removed from service. Section 47 of The Persons with Disabilities (Equal Opportunities, Protection of Rights and Full Participation) Act of 1995 provides that no employee afflicted with mental illness can be removed from service.

> Even if the petitioner was found suffering disability on account of mental illness, Section 47 of Disabilities Act makes it obligatory to provide suitable alternate employment on the same salary drawn before.

This was the first case in which Section 47 was considered.

Reference:

A. Tamilarasi vs. The District Collector, Tuticorin, 2007 (6) MLJ 425 = 2007 (4) LLN 452

Janaki, the intrepid grandmother

A paatti (Granny) called Janaki has her house twenty feet away from the temple on West Sannadhi Street, Kumbakonam, a temple town. All the houses on the street were built two feet above street level. There were two small steps at the entrance to her house. In 2005, the Kumbakonam municipality suddenly came to Janaki paatti's door to demolish the steps. When asked why, they explained that the High Court had ordered all encroachments within the municipality limits to be removed.

If the steps were demolished, Granny would become a virtual prisoner in her own house, unable to come and go easily due to her age. Janaki paatti wrote a letter about it to the Madurai bench of the Madras High Court. She said in her letter that she had no means to engage a lawyer and she requested the High Court to stop the municipality from demolishing the steps. She asked the little boy next door to post the letter and, leaving the rest to the Lord Sarangapani Perumal, she went on with her day. The High Court admitted her letter as a writ petition and issued a notice to the municipality. The court noted:

> Despite pleading with the authorities they have demolished the two steps which are the only means to get into her house. She also pleaded that she cannot engage a counsel and appear before this court for the restoration of the two steps ... Even in her letter she had stated that the length, width and height of

> the steps ... as 27 inches by 11 inches by 9 inches for one step and it was same for the second step. [I]t does not cause any harm or hindrance to any one.

The municipality filed its response after two and a half years. It stated that it was their duty to remove encroachments, and if the removal of small encroachments was prohibited, how could they remove the bigger ones. Not satisfied with this reply, the High Court directed them to file a photograph of West Sannadhi Street and also a map of the street. The map showed that the two steps occupied a space of 0.1748 sq. ft. (less than 0.25 sq. ft.) and that the street was twenty feet wide. In the photograph filed by the municipality it was seen that in front of Janaki Granny's house stood an electric pole in the middle of the street. One thing was clear to the High Court when it saw the map and photograph: the act of the municipality was mala fide and petty. There was no public interest served by the action. It merely wanted to punish the residents of Sannadhi Street. Further, the Sannadhi Street was not a thoroughfare, since the street ended at the temple.

The court stated:

> The Commissioner must be clear about his priorities. The devotees coming in their cars ... once in a while cannot be a ground to remove the two small steps from the front of the house of the old lady when it does not cause hardship or hindrance, as seen from the photographs. It is these people like the petitioner who live in the place for 365 days in a year. It is cruel to expect an old lady like the petitioner to climb up 2 ft. height to enter the house without there being any approach steps.

The High Court not only condemned the municipality, it also ordered that those two small steps must not be demolished. It directed the registry to send a copy of the judgment free of cost to the Granny.

No words of praise are enough for Janaki the Granny's intrepid act. In spite of her old age she fought for justice resourcefully, with just a postcard as her weapon.

Reference:

S. Janaki vs. The District Collector, Thanjavur, W.P. (MD) No. 2871 of 2005, dt. 10.9.2008

The problem with toilets

We are children of the Indus Valley Civilization. We can take pride in being the descendants of a people who constructed bathrooms and toilets 5,000 years ago. None of us would have passed our history test without reading about Mohenjodaro and Harappa. Sixty-two kilometres from Hyderabad in Pakistan, at a village called Lothal on the Indian side of the border, excavations uncovered sewage channels made of baked mud. The site of Harappa reveals bathrooms and toilets made of fired clay. The excavations in Mahenjodaro revealed that in the houses of the Dravidians of those times, there were attached toilets.

Oh, descendants of a glorious heritage! Tamil Nadu and the Tamil speaking people have fallen so low now! Why have you forgotten your history? Forty-two per cent of the people in the Asian–African countries have converted open spaces into toilets, while we continue to bear the burden of infectious diseases and health hazards that result from open defecation. A High Court asked such questions in a case. But let us examine another case, one concerning the toilets that do exist.

There is a district munsif court in Ambattur. Two thousand members of the public visit this court every day, of whom two hundred are lawyers and twenty work in the court. Suddenly, one day in November 2006, the doors of the toilets in the court premises were locked. No one knew why. Renuka Devi, a woman lawyer who suffered this torture for a week wrote a letter to the complaint section of a Tamil newspaper. I happened to read it and showed a translated version to the then Chief Justice, A.P. Shah. We took it on file as a writ petition and summoned the Commissioner of the Ambattur municipality. He appeared in court and offered his apology. His explanation was this: the municipality office had been shifted to a new building. 'The toilet was located in the old municipal office, which office was shifted subsequently to a new building. Since the person who had to maintain it had also been transferred, he locked the toilet and went away. This mistake was brought to my attention only after I received the notice from the High Court. Immediately I saw to it that the toilets were cleaned, the walls were white-washed and the water tanks were filled with water and I have handed over the keys to the court.' In forty-eight hours, the High Court solved the problem by taking prompt action suo motu. And it was all because a woman lawyer expressed her anguish through a letter to the editor of a newspaper.

Mahatma Gandhi said that India lives in her villages. But even today poor people living in thousands of villages have no proper toilet facilities. To set this problem right, schemes for building public toilets were framed in many villages with funds provided by the World Bank. Immediately, disputes arose regarding the location of the toilets, since people vehemently objected that they should not be put up near their homes. These objections were taken up as writ petitions by the High Court. It is impossible to list all the cases. I will give you one sample.

Ayodhyapattinam is a village in Salem district. The village panchayat resolved to build public toilets in the space available for use under the Anna Marumalarchi Scheme and the panchayat entrusted the job to a contractor. One Tamilarasi and two other villagers opposed it.

The Court heard the case, dismissed it and confirmed the

resolution of the Panchayat.[i] The court noted:

> [R]espondents have clearly demonstrated that there was a necessity to build toilets as there were 50 dalit families living in that area, and further, the land in question was grama natham land. Sufficient safeguards have been made to avoid any seepage and [the toilets are] being constructed with modern ideas. ... The petitioners' contention that the toilet was in the land owned by them is clearly found to be erroneous. ... The town panchayat is an elected body. Being conscious of the public need, especially of the dalits, they have passed a resolution unanimously to construct the toilets for needy people.

The court ordered that:

> It is not for the petitioners to forestall such efforts made by respondent Panchayat. Since the construction is in an advanced stage, the petitioners cannot challenge it on untenable grounds. The petitioners ... came forward to challenge the action of the town panchayat taken pursuant to the resolution. The contentions raised by the petitioners cannot be accepted.

It is indeed amazing that persons who live with attached bathrooms in their houses should oppose a scheme for construction of public toilets. This is the reason why this chapter commenced by asking why a country which is a cradle of civilization has fallen so low. The toilets had to be given police protection. In North Chennai, 225 toilets were constructed and maintained by the organization called Sulabh. However, the Chennai corporation cancelled the maintenance contract entered into with Sulabh. Immediately the members of the corporation who belonged to that area brought the toilets under their control and began to charge fees. The sanitary health workers opposed this and filed a case through their union. After hearing them, the Court ordered that the deputy commissioner of police should take control of the fifty-one toilets that were taken over illegally by the councillors and also ordered police protection to the toilets. A Tamil newspaper entertained itself by publishing a cartoon titled 'the toilet guardians'.

In the women's sub-jail—these are small establishments at the sub-divisional level—there are no toilet facilities and no privacy. A complaint was given in this regard to the Court. The Court took it up as a petition suo motu and appointed advocate Sudha Ramalingam as the advocate commissioner, directing her to visit the prisons of Tamil Nadu and file a report. Her report brought to light the darkness that prevailed in the jails of Tamil Nadu. On the basis of her report, the Court issued several directions to the government and prison authorities. One of them was the immediate construction of toilets with water facility in all sub-jails and the construction of four-feet-high compound walls with doors to ensure privacy.[ii] The government ordered the implementation of the Court's directions. There was a slight amelioration in the conditions of women prisoners.

An opinion poll conducted in USA asked respondents to name the greatest invention of the twentieth century. The answer was not nuclear power or television or satellites. The vote went to the invention of the modern toilet.

It is only because the then Chief Justice Gokhale (Madras High Court) understood the importance of toilets, that on International Women's Day (8 March 2010) a function was held in the court complex to inaugurate toilets. A newspaper carried it, together with photographs. Even so, it is a matter of distress that there are not enough restrooms for the public who come in their thousands to the courts. In 2015, the state of Haryana took the unprecedented step of bringing an amendment to the Panchayati Raj Act, saying that only those who have toilets at home can contest in panchayat elections. The Supreme Court has also held that this amendment is valid.

References:

i) *R. Tamilarasi vs. The District Collector*, 2010 (8) MLJ 662 = 2010 Writ LR 680

ii) Suo Motu Writ Petition No. 21243 of 2006, dt. 18.3.2007 (DB)

Durgamoorthi

Some years ago, a cell phone company published an advertisement which asked us to talk, talk, and keep talking. Ever since, our people have not stopped talking into their phones. A former union minister was severely criticized for commenting that her people who have no toilet facility are hankering after cell phones.

Mahakavi Bharathi spoke about Bharath Mata as one with thirty crore faces who upheld righteousness with her sixty crore hands. Today he would have sung that Mother India with her 120 crore faces and 240 crore hands spends multiple lifetimes talking into her cell phones. The population of Tamil Nadu is 7.21 crores, but judging from mobile phone usage you would imagine it was far greater.

Today a mobile phone is not just an instrument of spoken communication. It is a mini computer, a camera, a voice recorder, a calendar, an instrument which sends short messages and receives news. In addition, it is an alarm clock that also provides video games and daily news, and a radio, a music player and television.

It has become a very intimate friend for most people. But the courts have barred entry to cell phones. As early as 2005, the Gujarat High Court issued an order declaring that the use of cell phones while the court is in session amounts to contempt and users may be proceeded against if their cell phones obstruct court proceedings. The High Courts at Kerala (2001) and Karnataka (2000) have ordered that taking pictures of court proceedings is an act of contempt. If any of you entered a High Court today you would see notices such as: 'Mobile phones are prohibited'; 'If mobile phone is used it will be confiscated'; 'Mobile phone users will be proceeded against for contempt'. Just reading them can fill the heart with terror. Proceedings for contempt were initiated against a government servant who was recording a certain case on his cell phone. He fell at the feet of the judge and asked for forgiveness. After this incident, the government of Tamil Nadu issued a Government Order listing the rules to be followed by officials when they attend court.

Let us turn to the legal battle faced by Durgamoorthi, a revenue divisional officer (RDO). In 1961, Parliament enacted the Advocates Act. Section 30 of the Act says that legal practitioners have the right to appear before all courts, tribunals and officers empowered to record evidence. For reasons unknown, that section was not brought into force for fifty years. After several demonstrations by lawyers, it was finally implemented on 15 June 2011 by the then law minister Veerappa Moily. On the same day, lawyers in Madurai were on a boycott of the courts for entirely other reasons. (The boycott went on a few more days.) Durgamoorthi, RDO of Sivaganga, was present in Court no. 4 of the Madurai bench of the High Court. There was no crowd at court this day since there were no lawyers. The judge called out the list, adjourned the cases and retired to his chamber. While she was seated in court, Durga received a phone call from the collector. Her cell phone was on silent mode, and after conveying in a soft voice that she was in Madurai on court duty, she switched it off. A lawyer who was not in his robes was seated in the row ahead of Durga's. Using his cell phone, he took a picture of Durga speaking into hers. She objected to this. An argument broke out between her and the lawyer, which continued even after they had left the court.

The lawyer asked if Durga did not know that use of cell phones in the courtroom was an act of contempt. Durga replied that she was an executive magistrate as per the Code of Criminal Procedure and therefore she knew the rules perfectly well. She had taken an urgent call from the collector's office and hung up after saying she was in court. She was angry with the lawyer for taking a picture of her without permission, and having the cheek to accuse her of using a cell phone in court when he had committed the same act. There is nothing to indicate whether this was brought to the notice of the High Court or whether the court took any action in this regard.

After this incident, Durga received a notice from the affronted lawyer, Mr. Neelamegam. He informed her that she had committed contempt of court, that her conduct had caused him 'mental agony' and he would be initiating criminal proceedings against her. Durgamoorthi replied that she had committed no such thing, and if her use of a cell phone was to be treated as an act of contempt then the advocate who had photographed her also stood in contempt. She added that she was ready to face any criminal action he might bring against her.

On 30 June 2011 Neelamegam sent a complaint to the High Court, requesting it to initiate contempt proceedings against Durgamoorthi. He also filed a criminal complaint at the Othakkadai Police Station, at Madurai, that Durgamoorthi had abused him verbally and threatened him. Since no action was taken on his two complaints, he filed a contempt petition in the High Court. There are two kinds of contempt, civil and criminal. Refusal to abide by court orders is considered as civil contempt. Obstruction of court proceedings is a matter of criminal contempt. If a person uses a cell phone while the court is in session and disturbs the proceedings, then the judge, who is the presiding officer of the court, can immediately take suo motu notice and punish the contemnor. Otherwise, a person who files a petition for criminal contempt must get the written sanction of the advocate general. Since the petition filed by Neelamegam did not have this sanction, the registrar refused to take the case on file. The lawyer then complained to the Administrative Judge and thereafter the case was listed and Durgamoorthi was asked to appear in court. She appeared and offered her explanation. The court noted:

> [A]fter getting a legal notice from the petitioner, in admitting her mistake of using the cell phone—though for a brief period—and later when the contempt petition was filed, her expressing respect for the Court proceedings and tendering an unconditional apology will clearly show that she had never intended to commit any contempt, [still less] a criminal contempt for tending to obstruct the administration in the course of justice. In view of the above, the contempt petition must necessarily fail. Accordingly, it is liable to be dismissed.

After hearing both sides, the Judge dismissed the contempt proceedings. The court also condemned the lawyer for photographing Durgamoorthi with his cell phone. In its order the court held that the use of cell phones is often necessary for lawyers while in court and unless it obstructs court proceedings, mere use may not be held to be an offence. Durgamoorthi heaved a sigh of relief upon being absolved.

Reference:

K. Neelamegam vs. Ms. Durgamoorthi, 2012 (1) CTC 246

Kasthuri

'*Charkha chala-chala ke swarajya lenge*' was the vibrant chant of our freedom fighters. It means that spinning khadi would take us to independence. The tragedy is what happened after we attained freedom. Khadi, a symbol of our thirst for freedom, the khadi which was worn casting aside foreign fabric, now came to be treated with contempt along with the thirst for freedom that it stands for.

Justice V.R. Krishna Iyer of the Supreme Court always wore khadi, a white khadi shirt and dhoti, and on his feet he wore rubber slippers. A friend in Chennai once invited him to dinner at the Madras Cricket Club (MCC). But the watchman did not let him enter the club. The mandatory dress code at the club was western clothes: trousers and shirt. Though the host argued with the watchman and even mentioned that his guest was a retired judge of the Supreme Court, the watchman said this was a club rule and could not be breached. Justice Krishna Iyer felt a distaste at this exchange and requested the watchman to bring him the visitor's book. Krishna Iyer wrote a few words in the book and left the scene.

> I came as a Guest for Dinner but was stopped by the janitor at the MCC entrance because I was not wearing Western Costume, the only permissible apparel according to the MCC culture. Alas! Swaraj has made the country free but has

> stopped at the doorsteps of the MCC. I return without [my] dinner but as a proud Indian.

This incident shows the persistence of the colonial hangover. Our Constitution was amended in 1976. This introduced fundamental duties for every citizen. Article 51-A(b) says it is the duty of every citizen of India to 'cherish and follow the noble ideals which inspired our national struggle for freedom'.

For a private body to act in violation of our fundamental duties is bad enough. Shall we see how a public authority went after its employee, Kasthuri, all because she followed her fundamental duty?

The airports in India were initially administered by the Ministry of Civil Aviation. In 1985, Parliament enacted the Airports Authority Act. The Airports Authority of India was formed and all airports were brought under the Public Works Department in 1986. Kasthuri was a senior office assistant at the Chennai office of the Airports Authority. Drawn to Gandhiji's ideals since childhood, she had taken an oath to wear only khadi or handloom throughout her life.

In 1994, the Airports Authority of India prescribed uniforms for its employees. The uniforms were of a synthetic silk or polyester fabric. Though the uniforms were mandatory, there was no rule regarding the fabric. Kasthuri refused to collect the uniforms from the office. In 1996, the authority ordered her to collect the regulation sarees and start wearing them. Kasthuri sent a letter asking for permission to continue wearing khadi or handloom fabric of the shade or colour prescribed by the Department. She received no reply and she continued to wear khadi sarees to office. In August 1999, the office directed her to wear the polyester uniform distributed by the office. If she did not, she was warned that disciplinary proceedings would be initiated against her. The letter stated:

> This is considered as most indisciplined behaviour and a serious lapse on the part of the official. In this regard, attention of Kum. Kasturi is drawn to Regulation 5(24) of NAA (ECDA) Regulations, 1988, according to which, non-wearing of uniform while on duty by any employee of the Authority constitutes a serious misconduct and attracts initiation of disciplinary proceedings . . . Further, she will not be allowed to attend her duties without wearing of uniform.

She filed a writ petition against this order, in 1999, and a judgment was given in her favour on 5 November 2008.

That judgment referred to Gandhiji's struggle to boycott foreign goods. Mahatma Gandhi said that spinning our own yarn would help create more employment. The cotton produced in our country was taken by the British to Lancashire (England) and brought back as finished goods for sale in this country. If we refused to buy it, the British would suffer. He wanted every Indian to pledge that they would wear only khadi. 'Boycott British Goods' became our national slogan. Gandhiji wrote extensively on the use of khaddar and devoted large space in his newspaper, *Harijan*, to this subject. In 1936, two Gandhians wrote to him from Bihar. They quoted Pandit Jawaharlal Nehru as saying that khadi would continue till independent India achieved complete industrialization, and wanted to know Gandhiji's views. Gandhiji replied by stating in the *Harijan* (4 July 1936) that the wearing of khadi would continue regardless of whether India became industrialized or not.

The High Court condemned the attitude of the Authority which was ignorant of the history of khadi, and said that it had acted vindictively against Kasthuri. The Court found that the Authority was violating fundamental duties and set aside the disciplinary proceedings launched against Kasthuri, terming them 'sartorial despotism'. The Court further imposed costs of Rs. 5,000 on the Authority for not respecting Kasthuri's spirit.

The newspapers reported this case extensively, the *Times of India* even published a cartoon on the first page. When he heard about this judgment Justice Krishna Iyer wrote a letter describing the judgment as one drenched in patriotism.

We cannot but praise Kasthuri for fighting against her employer's autocracy with courage. After this, there was an incident in the Tamil Nadu Cricket Association, when a High Court judge was not permitted to enter its premises because he was wearing a khaddar dhoti and shirt. There was strong protest against this. The State Assembly passed the Tamil Nadu Entry into Public Places (Removal of Restriction on Dress) Act, 2014, which made it punishable with imprisonment for a private body to refuse entry to a person wearing a dhoti. It is heartening to hear that now even Air India permits its employees to wear khadi.

Reference:

S. Kasthuri vs. The Chairman, Airports Authority of India, 2009 (2) LLN 178

Umadevi

Love is blind, they say. But often it is the police force that has neither eyes nor respect for others.

In Chennai, we read news about how the policemen behave without any decency, and even extort money from lovers on the Marina beach. Many of these policemen have turned into culture vigilantes, frowning on lovers and couples who meet in public places like parks.

A policeman on the Marina who had appointed himself protector of culture so exceeded his limits that he had to be temporarily relieved of his duties. This action was possible because the affected parties were lawyers. If they had been ordinary people . . . ?

If cultural vigilantism by policemen in public spaces was not bad enough, the tragic story of Umadevi and Krishnan tells us how a married couple could be arrested under the Immoral Traffic (Prevention) Act while they were in their private space, a proceeding that also put their government jobs in jeopardy.

Umadevi was an Anganwadi worker in Thiruvonam Municipality, Thanjavur district, Tamil Nadu. At the time of this occurrence she was thirty-five. She came from an economically sound background and was not married. Krishnan, the headmaster of the elementary school there, was fifty-one years old and had lost his wife six years earlier. His son lived abroad and his daughter lived in her marital home. Uma married him in May 2006, against the wishes of her family. In July, their marriage was registered in the Registrar's office, Thiruvaiyaru, Tamil Nadu.

Later they travelled to Kumbakonam, Swamimalai, and also to Thanjavur—to attend a relative's marriage—and on this trip they received a horrifying shock from the police. It happened when they were staying at a private boarding place. One of the odd-jobs persons there did double duty as a police informer. Based on information received from him, the police inspector, one Vasanta, hurried to the lodge along with the Immoral Traffic (Prevention) squad, arrested the couple and produced them in court. Without any application of mind, the magistrate automatically remanded them to custody.

Umadevi spent seven days in the women's jail, Trichy, and Krishnan spent five days in Thanjavur Jail. They were then let out on bail. In the meantime, their pictures had appeared in the newspapers, as persons arrested in a prostitution case thanks to the 'diligence' of the police. The diligent police force had also diligently informed the respective authorities under whom the couple worked. Whereupon both were removed from service. They faced humiliation at the workplace, at home, amongst family members and everywhere that they were known.

Despite such humiliation, Umadevi was unfazed. She was determined to prove her innocence to the whole world. She approached the Madurai bench of the Madras High Court. The High Court granted an interim stay on the orders of termination to both Umadevi and Krishnan. Notices were sent asking the State and the police department to explain their conduct. The reply from her superior, the child welfare officer, was breathtakingly self-assured. He stated: 'Umadevi is an unmarried woman. She was staying with a man in a lodging house. So she was arrested under the Immoral Traffic Act. Therefore her services were terminated.'

Even though the Supreme Court (1994) has held that the power to terminate subordinates must not be exercised by government officials arbitrarily and mechanically, very few officers bear this in mind.

The High Court severely reprimanded the police officers for arresting the married couple under the Immoral Traffic (Prevention) Act, 1956, and condemned the superiors who had terminated their employment. The court noted:

> The police are only a law enforcing force and they cannot assume that the duty [extends] to moral policing. The raiding party from the All women Police Force by their conduct had brought not only misery to two consenting individuals who were legally wedded as husband and wife but also brought disrepute to their life, especially [as they were] working in remote villages. The loss of face and defamation caused by the overenthusiastic police can never be condoned nor can the petitioners be compensated suitably ... Further, between two consenting individuals found in a room in any posture in a private lodge, no criminal act can be alleged ... to make it a penal offence.

It restored the husband and wife in service with full back wages. The Court expressed its regret that it was unable to remove the social humiliation suffered by them. It held that the police had no power to arrest a person based on a false complaint or to peek through the keyhole of a closed room.

Umadevi's courage and success in fighting against the chastity vigilantes must be applauded.

Reference:

Uma @ Umadevi vs. The District Collector, Thanjavur, W.P. (MD) No. 11138 of 2006, dt. 4.10.2007

